BROADENING
YOUR BIBLICAL
HORIZONS
NEW TESTAMENT SURVEY

By

WALTER M. DUNNETT, Ph.D.

Professor of Bible
Northwestern College
Roseville, Minnesota

EVANGELICAL TRAINING ASSOCIATION

110 Bridge Street, Box 327
Wheaton, Illinois 60189

20 19 18
0 9 8 7 6 5

First Edition

Library of Congress catalog and card number: 63-7410

ISBN 0-910566-03-8

Preface

"Tell me, sir," the sincere young woman inquired anxiously of the preacher, "What is the Bible all about?" After serious thought the preacher replied, "My girl, the Bible is all about Jesus."

That, essentially, is the message of the New Testament. It is all about Jesus. From the story of the humble birth in Bethlehem as recorded in the Gospels, to the scene of the glorious exaltation as King of Kings and Lord of Lords as depicted in the book of Revelation, the subject is the same. At the beginning of his study of the New Testament, the student will do well to look for the Lord Jesus Christ and His teachings.

Before a study of the books of the New Testament is undertaken in systematic fashion, two preliminary matters of great importance must be considered. The New Testament has a background which, when properly considered, will help to illuminate the books themselves. Chapter I, therefore, deals with the three most important areas of this setting: the Hebrew, the Greek, and the Roman. Following this treatment, the chapter presents an overview, or "bird's eye view," of the whole New Testament. This approach, sometimes called the "synthetic," is vital to acquaint the student with the major divisions or parts of the New Testament and the unity of the whole.

Having completed chapter one, you, the student, are ready to investigate each book separately. Chapters II through XII consider the respective writers and their writings — the purpose, outline, main content, and leading features.

The attention of the reader is called to *Additional Exploration* and *Suggested Resources* sections which appear at the end of each chapter in the book. These serve at least a dual purpose: (1) they provide opportunity for you to carry on your studies in a more detailed and intensive manner whenever you wish to do so; (2) they provide information regarding matters which could be given only passing mention. For instance, in the study of the Gospels, the so-called "Synoptic Problem" demands careful investigation. For such a study, books on New Testament Introduction, Bible dictionaries, and detailed commentaries will prove useful. A list of resource books is contained in an inexpensive bibliography published by Evangelical Teacher Training Association.

In addition, the maps and charts which are included are for the purpose of illustrating and integrating the New Testament materials. Use them as you encounter them in the various chapters. The same may be said for the outlines. They are meant to be guides in the study of each book. And you will find that the questions at the end of the chapters will be valuable for testing your grasp of the materials which you have studied.

The text of the American Standard Version, 1901, has been used in most citations from the New Testament. It stands as one of the best study Bibles available.

Thanks are due to Moody Press, Chicago, for their kind permission given to use materials from my book, *An Outline of New Testament Survey,* 1960. The outlines, charts, and one quotation in Chapter XI have been taken from that work.

On then to study. May it be done in the spirit of II Timothy 2:15, and result in the enrichment of the life of all who undertake the task at hand.

WALTER M. DUNNETT

"Study to shew thyself approved unto God,
a workman that needeth not to be ashamed,
rightly dividing the word of truth."
—II TIMOTHY 2:15

Contents

CHAPTER ONE

Background and Composition

of the New Testament

The world of the New Testament was a busy and exciting one. All roads led to Rome; the Caesars held sway across most of the inhabited earth; in a tiny town of Palestine One was born who was to change the world! Following the time of Christ on earth, the Christian Church emerged, beginning as a small band of men and women, then growing to a great multitude of people. To instruct local congregations of believers and to inform them of the life and teachings of Christ, the books of the New Testament were written.

But these events did not come about suddenly. They were the result of preparation—and that by God Himself! "When the fulness of the time came, God sent forth His Son" (Gal. 4:4). In the years that preceded the coming of Christ, God had been active in the lives of men and in the affairs of nations. Many had a part in this pre-Christian era. Among the three most important contributors were the Hebrews and their religion; the Greeks and their language; and the Romans and their social and political organization.

THE HEBREW PREPARATION Chosen by God as "a kingdom of priests, and a holy nation" (Exod. 19:6), the people of Israel were in a position of privilege. They were to be the messengers of the Lord to the nations around them. But they failed! Because of almost continuous disobedience and the gross sin of idolatry, God's judgment fell with finality upon them in the year 587 B.C. and the nation was carried away captive by Nebuchadnezzar into the land of Babylon.

From this center of captivity they were progressively scattered across the ancient world. This crucial event, called The Great Dispersion, left its effects upon the Hebrew people. But as they went, and wherever they went, many of them let it be known that they were worshipers of the one true God, Jehovah. Two emphases in particular, monotheism (the belief in only one God) and the Law of God, stood out in the midst of pagan societies.

So it was, in later years, when Christ was born and when the apostolic proclamations went forth, the way had been prepared. The words, the ideas, the message itself was not entirely new. And not only had people heard the message, but they had read it too. The Hebrew Old Testament was translated into Greek in the city of Alexandria in Egypt between the years

250-150 B.C. As Greek was then the common language of the world, this translation, called the Septuagint (meaning "the Seventy"), made the Old Testament teachings available to all who could read.

Sometime during the second century B.C., the major sects, or parties, among the Jews seem to have had their origin. As one reads the historical books of the New Testament (Matthew through Acts), the names of the Pharisees and the Sadducees often appear. The Pharisees were the larger of the two groups and were predominantly the students and teachers of the Old Testament, while the Sadducees were the powerful political leaders, including the high priests and leading officials of the Jerusalem Sanhedrin (which was composed of seventy plus the high priest).

One is impressed with the orthodox character of the Pharisees. They firmly maintained the sacred character of the entire Old Testament, taught belief in the resurrection and the judgment of the last day, and affirmed the existence of angels and spirits. These tenets the Sadducees denied (Acts 23:6-8). Yet it was the former group which most often came under the condemnation of the Lord Jesus in His teaching—not because they failed to be orthodox, but because they emphasized the unimportant and neglected the weightier elements of the Law (Matt. 23:23, 24).

THE GREEK PREPARATION   One language and one world! That was the ambition of young Alexander, the son of King Philip of Macedon more than three hundred years before the birth of Christ. His ambition was largely realized between the years 334-323 B.C. Sweeping across the ancient world, like lightning across the sky, Alexander soon conquered it. To cement his victories he established the Greek language as the *lingua franca,* the common tongue, and the Greek culture as the pattern of thought and life. Although his vast empire quickly disintegrated after his premature death, the results were of long standing.

How did these third-century happenings relate to the coming of Christianity and the New Testament? A matchless vehicle of expression for the Christian message was provided. The apostolic preaching was done largely in Greek; the New Testament books were written in Greek, the common language of the world. Using the vocabulary of their day, the writers filled the words with new and significant meaning designed to convey the message of spiritual life to their readers. Such important terms as *Christ, redeem, ransom, church, wisdom,* and *word* illustrate this.

THE ROMAN PREPARATION   Above all else Rome was noted for her insistence upon law and order. The world was organized into a great empire extending from the Western end of the Mediterranean Sea to the Euphrates River in the Near East. By means of provinces and districts closely supervised by local governors. the empire was efficiently administered.

In the providence of God, the Romans prepared the world for the coming of Christianity in a number of ways.

First, the emphasis on law and order, backed by superior military might, made possible the days of peace during the reign of Caesar Augustus. It was during these days, says Luke the historian, that Mary brought forth her firstborn son (Luke 2:1-7) in the tiny village of Bethlehem in the Roman province of Judea.

Again, the Roman system of roads contributed greatly to the measure of ease and safety by which travelers could make their way back and forth across the empire. These roads were well paved, well drained, and usually patrolled. Paul traveled on such important roads as the Egnatian Way across Achaia and Macedonia and the Appian Way leading to Rome.

Another important factor, though negative in character, was the marked degeneration of morality and religion, and the deep longing for redemption found among the peoples of the Mediterranean Basin. They had lost faith in the ancient gods. The state religions were too formal and rigid to satisfy personal longings. The current philosophies of the day, likewise, lacked in real vigor and failed to appeal to the common man. Both in the East and the West the so-called "mystery cults" arose to offer personal salvation, fellowship with the gods, and the observance of secret rites.

Into this scene came Christianity proclaiming salvation, forgiveness, and peace. Centered in the historical incidents of the life, death, and resurrection of Jesus Christ, Christianity supplied the answer to man's spiritual need and moral void.

FIRST-CENTURY PALESTINE The principal ruling family in Palestine in the years which saw the dawn of the Christian era was the Herodian dynasty. Herod the Great was appointed by the Romans as the king of the Jews, reigning from 37 to 4 B.C. His rule was marked by intrigue and bloodshed, including the incident recorded in Matthew 2, called "the slaughter of the infants."

Of the sons of Herod the most noted in the Gospel records was Herod Antipas who ruled from 4 B.C. to A.D. 39 as Tetrarch of Galilee and Perea. It was this Herod who John the Baptizer accused of wrongfully marrying Herodias, which accusation cost John his life (Matt. 14:1-12). Jesus called Herod "that fox" (Luke 13:32) and it was he who was involved in the trial of Christ in Jerusalem (Luke 23:7-12).

Herod Agrippa I, the son of Aristobulus and grandson of Herod the Great, succeeded Antipas and ruled over Galilee, Samaria, and Judea. His reign, from A.D. 37-44, was cut short by his sudden death. Acts 12 records his murder of James the son of Zebedee and the imprisonment of Peter together with a cryptic account of Herod's death (vv. 21-23).

The last of the family to reign was Herod Agrippa II (A.D. 50-100). He appears in Acts 25 and 26 in conjunction with the trial of Paul before Festus in Caesarea. He, along with Festus, rendered a verdict of acquittal (26:31, 32).

Among the Roman procurators of Judea in the first century, Pontius Pilate (A.D. 26-36) is most notable as far as the New Testament record is concerned. Because of his share in the trial of Christ and his condemnation of the Lord after repeatedly rendering the verdict of "not guilty" (John 18:38—19:6), Pilate has attained unusual notoriety in history. Shortly after the death of Christ, he was deposed by Tiberius for an attack on the Samaritans and was ordered to appear before the emperor (A.D. 36). What actually happened to Pilate after this is uncertain.

Amid these political circumstances, the Jews were ruled directly by their own high priest and his cohorts in the Great Sanhedrin in Jerusalem. Three of these high priests are mentioned in the New Testament. Annas, the high-priest emeritus, was the father-in-law to Caiaphas, the ruling high priest at the time of the trial of Christ (John 18:13); Ananias appears in Acts 23:2.

The religious life of the Jews was centered in the Temple in Jerusalem. This structure, called "Herod's Temple," was in process of completion during the time of Christ (cf. John 2:20). It had as its antecedents the temples of Solomon and Zerubbabel and was the symbol of their religious hopes and aspirations. From near and far the people came to worship, offer sacrifices, and observe the religious festivals of Judaism, especially the feasts of Passover, Pentecost, and Tabernacles.

Side by side with the Temple in the religious life of Judaism was the synagogue. Especially to all those at a distance from Jerusalem, the synagogue was a substitute for the Temple. There were a number of synagogues even in Jerusalem. They were primarily places of instruction and prayer for the Jews and Gentile adherents of the Jewish faith. The Scripture was read, commented on, and at various places in the service prayers were offered. Both Jesus and the early Christians frequented the synagogue (Luke 4:16-30; Acts 13:14 ff.; 26:11).

To the Jew, the Old Testament was the Book of God. God was One, the Law was the revelation of His will, life was under His jurisdiction. There was an air of expectancy that God would intervene and save His people (Luke 2:25). So it was when Christ was born, He came into a world prepared —"in the fulness of the time." The New Testament complements the Old Testament, carrying on and completing the record of God's revelation, and clarifying to the Jew, the Gentile, and the Church of God the eternal truths of the living God.

COMPOSITION OF THE NEW TESTAMENT   The New Testament contains twenty-seven books which may be classified into three major groups based on their literary characteristics. The accompanying chart briefly presents the books, their authors, and the approximate dates of writing.

Chronological division

Many scholars hold James to be the earliest book of the New Testament, written about A.D. 45.[1] Aside from the question of the place of James, it is practically certain that some of Paul's letters represent the first written records of the early Church. Galatians is regarded by some to have been written as early as A.D. 47/48. The Thessalonian Epistles are from the early

The New Testament Literature

Literary Type	Titles	Approximate Date Written*	Writers
		A.D.	
Historical Literature (5)	Matthew	55-70	Matthew
	Mark	50-68	Mark
	Luke	60	Luke
	John	85-95	John
	Acts	62	Luke
Epistolary Literature (21)	Romans	55/56	
	I Corinthians	55	
	II Corinthians	56	
	Galatians	48/49 to 57/58	
	Ephesians	60/61	
	Philippians	61	
	Colossians	60/61	
	I Thessalonians	50/51	Paul
	II Thessalonians	51	
	I Timothy**	63	
	II Timothy**	67	
	Titus**	65	
	Philemon**	60/61	
	Hebrews	65-70	Anonymous
	James	45	James
	I Peter	63-65	Peter
	II Peter	65-67	
	I John	85-90	John
	II John**	85-90	
	III John**	85-90	
	Jude	67/68 to 80-85	Jude
Prophetical Literature (1)	Revelation	90-95	John

[1] Others place the epistle later, about A.D. 62. If the early date is correct, it would give a date of only about 15 years after the death of Christ.
*Though Bible scholars differ in the exact date when written, these dates cover approximate calculations.
**Written to individuals.

ministry of Paul the missionary, written from Corinth before or during the time of Gallio (cf. Acts 18:12-17; I Thess. 3:1-10), which would mean A.D. 50 or 51. These early writings give an insight into the character of the Christian message and of the Christians themselves. Especially important in this regard are passages such as Galatians 1:6—2:21; 6:11-17; I Thessalonians 1:2-10; 2:13-16; II Thessalonians 2:1-12; 3:6-15.

In contrast to these writings, those of John the Apostle constitute the last of the books to be written. According to tradition, as well as indications in the books themselves, John's works reflect problems being faced by the Church near the end of the first century. His major writings deal mainly with aspects of salvation: the Gospel, the *nature* of salvation; the First Epistle, the *assurance* of salvation; and the Revelation, the *consummation* of salvation.

Literary division

While the literary divisions of the New Testament do not follow a chronological scheme, they do reflect the logical order of God's program. First, the Gospels and Acts constitute the basic history which is necessary for a proper understanding and appreciation of the later works. The life of Christ and the origin of the Church is foundational. The story of the Founder is required before one regards the superstructure which was erected. The Church is "built upon the foundation of the apostles and prophets, Christ Jesus himself being the chief corner stone" (Eph. 2:20).

Matthew—the introduction to "Jesus Christ, the King of the Jews." Herein is recorded the fulfillment of many of the Old Testament prophecies with the coming of the Messiah. The teaching of Christ is emphasized.

Mark—the picture of Jesus as "the Servant of the Lord." He is busy about His Father's work, thus Mark emphasizes the activity, and especially the redemptive activity, of Christ.

Luke—the portrait of Jesus as "the Son of Man," the perfect representative of humanity. His life was given "to seek and to save that which was lost" (19:10). The sympathy and graciousness of Christ are emphasized.

A Harmony of the Ministry of Jesus

Gospel	The Period of Preparation	The Period of Public Ministry		The Period of Suffering	The Period of Triumph
		Opening	Closing		
Matthew	1:1—4:16	4:17—16:20	16:21—26: 2	26:3—27:66	28:1-20
Mark	1:1—13	1:14—8:30	8:31—13:37	14:1—15:47	16:1-20
Luke	1:1—4:13	4:14—9:21	9:22—21:38	22:1—23:56	24:1-53
John	1:1—34	1:35—6:71	7: 1—12:50	13:1—19:42	20:1—21:25

John—the presentation of Jesus as "the Son of God," the eternal Word who came to reveal God to man. This Gospel emphasizes the relation of Christ to those around Him—the personal contacts which changed the lives of those who met Him. By the true realization of His divine Sonship, eternal life was received.

Acts—this is the continuation of Luke's Gospel and presents the Risen Christ working through His apostles who had been empowered by the Holy Spirit. The origin of the Church, the Body of Christ, and its expansion "unto the uttermost part of the earth" is the theme of this first church history.

Then, the New Testament Epistles give the interpretation of the person and work of Christ, and apply His teachings to the lives of believers. The majority of these letters, at least thirteen, were penned by the Apostle Paul. Most of them are written in letter form. Of the twenty-one, all have names attached to them except Hebrews and the three Epistles of John.

Nine of the Pauline writings were sent to churches; four to individuals. Most of them deal with problem situations then existing in the churches (Ephesians seems to be an exception). Some are very personal in tone (Philippians and II Corinthians); others appear to have a more formal, almost thesis-like style, and in their main features (excluding the usual personal introduction and conclusion) show a rather businesslike tone. Romans would probably be the outstanding example of this type. Further, the letters of Paul show great variety in content, and also combine doctrinal and practical components in good balance.

The remaining epistles, while varied in authorship, may be conveniently grouped under two main headings. Some deal primarily with the problem of suffering (Hebrews, James, and I Peter), while the rest treat mainly the problem of false teaching (I and II Peter, I, II, and III John and Jude). Both these problems became increasingly serious as the first century progressed. Persecution came first from Jewish opponents and later (after A.D. 64) from the Roman government. Christ had warned His followers of the rise of false Christs and false prophets (Matt. 24:24), and Paul had said much the same thing to the elders of the Ephesian Church (Acts 20:29, 30). By the time John wrote his letters, the Gnostics (teachers who claimed to possess a superior philosophical-religious type of knowledge) were plaguing the Church. His epistles were an answer to that error.

Finally, there is the well-known prophetical writing in the New Testament, the Revelation (or Apocalypse, the unveiling) of Jesus Christ. Like the prophecy of Daniel in the Old Testament, this book deals, for the most part, with the judgments of God in the last days upon "those that dwell upon the earth." In Revelation, the climax of redemption is portrayed. The earlier word of Paul, that God's purpose was "to sum up all things in Christ" (Eph. 1:10), is realized as John writes, "The kingdom of the world is become *the kingdom* of our Lord, and of His Christ: and he shall reign for ever and ever" (Rev. 11:15).

And so the New Testament has come to us. "God, having of old time spoken unto the fathers in the prophets by divers portions and in divers manners, hath at the end of these days spoken unto us in *his* Son" (Heb. 1:1, 2).

Word to the Student

Three types of review emphases are possible through utilizing the question and project sections at the end of each chapter. The first section contains direct questions and discussion suggestions. The direct questions are content centered and each is answered in the text content. In review, the student will benefit by studying these questions and also by formulating additional similar questions.

The discussion suggestions in the first section are also closely related to the text and may be profitably used for subjective review and fuller appreciation of the lesson content.

The first section should be used by the student in determining the measure of increased knowledge resultant from this study.

Additional exploration questions and projects are meant as guides for the student to apply the chapter teachings and to investigate related or more specific subjects.

The purpose and benefit of review activities will be realized only to the measure that the student uses them.

Suggested Questions and Discussions

1. Discuss the significant contributors and their contributions leading to the coming of Christ and the writing of the New Testament.
2. In what important ways did the Jewish Dispersion prepare the way for Christianity?
3. How did the Greek language and culture relate to Christianity?
4. In what ways did the Roman Empire contribute to the rise and spread of Christianity?
5. Distinguish between the Pharisees and the Sadducees. Which group is more prominent in the Gospels?
6. Name the three literary divisions of the New Testament and list the books included in each division.
7. Compare John's dealing with the subject of salvation in his Gospel, the First Epistle, and the Revelation.
8. How do the Gospels and the Acts lay the foundation for the remaining New Testament writings?
9. In what ways do the Epistles deal with the life and teachings of Christ?
10. How does the book of Revelation present Christ?

Additional Exploration

1. To get a clearer view of Christ in the New Testament, prepare a simple chart to use throughout the class sessions, listing the various aspects of His character and work. For example:

PORTRAITS OF CHRIST

His Character	*His Work*
Model Sufferer, Luke 23:34	Saviour, Luke 2:11
Sinless One, Luke 4	Teacher, Matt. 5

2. As the class sessions develop, list specific qualities in Christ's life desirable in your own life.

3. Refer to several good Bible commentaries or dictionaries for further background studies in preparation for a deeper understanding of the New Testament. In commentaries, background information is generally given prior to verse by verse comments.

Suggested Resources

ALEXANDER, DAVID and PAT, eds. *Eerdmans Handbook to the Bible*. Grand Rapids: Eerdmans Publishing Co., 1973.

BRUCE, F.F. *New Testament History*. Garden City, NY: Doubleday, 1972.

GEISLER, N. and NIX, W. *From God to Us: How We Got Our Bible*. Chicago: Moody Press, 1974.

HALLEY, HENRY H. *Halley's Bible Handbook*. Rev. ed. Grand Rapids: Zondervan Pub. House, 1976.

METZGER, B. M. *New Testament: Its Background, Growth and Content*. Nashville: Abingdon, 1965.

SCROGGIE, W. GRAHAM. *A Guide to the Gospels*. Old Tappan, NJ: Fleming H. Revell Co. (Pickering & Inglis), 1975.

TENNEY, MERRILL C. *New Testament Survey*. Rev. ed. Grand Rapids: Eerdmans Publishing Co., 1961.

THOMAS R. and GUNDRY, S., eds. *A Harmony of the Gospels with Explanations and Essays*. Chicago: Moody Press, 1978.

CHAPTER TWO

The Synoptic Gospels

Matthew, Mark, Luke

The first three Gospels are called the Synoptic Gospels because they "see together" or have the same point of view with regard to the life of Christ. They present the life of Christ in a way which complements the picture given in the Gospel of John.

The approach to the subject here will be twofold: first, the distinctive features of each Gospel; second, the common features of the three Gospels. That is to say, what are the characteristics which cause each book to differ from the others and what are the common characteristics found in all three books?

The Gospel of Matthew

SUGGESTED READING   Matthew 1—7, 13, 16, 24, 25, 28

AUTHOR   Matthew, one of the original disciples of Christ, wrote the first book in the New Testament. He was first named Levi and worked as a publican collecting taxes in Palestine until he was called to follow Jesus (9:9, 10; Mark 2:14, 15).

PURPOSE AND CONTENT   Matthew addressed his Gospel primarily to Jewish readers and presented Jesus as the Messiah, the King of the Jews. This is seen in such passages as His genealogy (1:1-17); the visit of the Magi (2:1-12); His entry into Jerusalem (21:5); the judgment of the nations (25:31-46); and, in common with the other Gospels, the superscription over the Cross (27:37). In addition to these statements, there is much in this first Gospel concerning "the kingdom of heaven." This expression is used by Matthew alone.

This book also serves as the bridge between the Old and the New Testaments. It links together the prophecies of the coming Messiah with the fulfillment of prophecy in the person of the Lord Jesus. Matthew often alludes to or quotes from the prophets and connects their words with his Subject. Of particular importance are such passages as 1:22, 23; 2:15, 17, 18, 23; 4:14, 16; 8:17; 12:17, 21; 13:35; 21:4, 5; 26:54, 56; 27:9. It is as though Matthew first notes the Old Testament which says, "He is coming," then presents his own message which says, "He is here!"

The discourses of Christ

The prominence of the discourses of Christ is easily observed in this Gospel. Matthew's pattern, as may be seen clearly in the outline of the book, is to include narrative material about Christ. Then follows an important discourse. There are five in the book, one in each of the five major divisions:

1. The Sermon on the Mount (5:1—7:29).
2. The Commission to the Twelve (10:1-42).
3. The Parables of the Kingdom (13:1-53).
4. The Meaning of Greatness and Forgiveness (18:1-35).
5. The Olivet Discourse (24:1—25:46).

In one way or another, each of these discourses relates to the claims which the King makes upon those who would share in His kingdom.

Outline

In the light of the dominant theme of this Gospel, then, the following outline will aid the student in his progress through the book. The clue to Matthew's structure is given by the fivefold repetition of the expression "when Jesus had finished" (7:28; 11:1; 13:53; 19:1; 26:1). This phrase marks the end of each major division of the Gospel. Together with the introduction (1:1—4:11) and the two concluding sections (26:3—28:15; 28:16-20), these five divisions form the complete record.

     I. The Introduction of the King, 1:1—4:11
    II. The Demands of the King, 4:12—7:29
   III. The Deeds of the King, 8:1—11:1
   IV. The Program of the King, 11:2—13:53
    V. The Destiny of the King, 13:54—19:2
   VI. The Problems of the King, 19:3—26:2
  VII. The Death and Resurrection of the King, 26:3—28:15
 VIII. The Final Commission by the King, 28:16-20

The Gospel of Mark

SUGGESTED READING   Mark 1, 2, 4, 6, 8—10, 13

AUTHOR   In contrast to Matthew, Mark was not one of the original disciples of Christ. He was, however, a native of Jerusalem (Acts 12:12), a companion of Simon Peter (I Pet. 5:13) and the cousin of Barnabas (Col. 4:10, ASV) who, in turn, was a close associate of Paul and the Jerusalem apostles. His relationship to the apostles was, therefore, close enough to render him familiar with the life of Christ and the activies of the early Christian group.

In A.D. 112, Papias cited Mark as "the interpreter of Peter." A comparison of Peter's sermon in Acts 10:34-43 with Mark's Gospel shows the former to be an outline of the life of Jesus which Mark has given in much greater detail.

PURPOSE   Mark addressed his Gospel primarily to Roman readers
AND CONTENT and presented Jesus as the Worker, the Servant of Jeho-
                  vah. (According to tradition, Mark wrote his record of
the life of Christ in Rome.) The chief characteristic of Christ in this book
is His activity, the mark of a good servant. The Greek word *eutheos,* translated variously as "straightway," "immediately," "anon," or "forthwith,"
appears forty-two times in the book. This message made a natural appeal
to the busy, practical Roman reader.

According to the amount of space which Mark allots to it, the most
important activity of Christ was His death and resurrection. About three-
eighths of the entire book is devoted to the narrative of the Passion Week
(the last week of the life of Christ, 11:1—16:18). In the story of a life,
this is a most striking feature, and shows clearly what aspect of His life was
considered by the Gospel writers to be of supreme concern.

OUTLINE   In keeping with the theme of the activity of Christ, the outline
                treats His life as a series of tours as He carried on His ministry.
By so doing, one is impressed with the continual "busyness" of the Servant
of Jehovah.

     I. Introduction, 1:1
     II. Preparatory Events, 1:2-13
     III. First Tour of Galilee, 1:14—4:34
          Miracles and Parables
     IV. Tour of Decapolis, 4:35—5:43
     V. Second Tour of Galilee, 6:1-29
     VI. Retreat to the Desert, 6:30-52
     VII. Third Tour of Galilee, 6:53—7:23
     VIII. Tour of the North Country, 7:24—9:29
          First announcement of Passion, (8:31)
     IX. Fourth Tour of Galilee, 9:30-50
          Second announcement of Passion, (9:31)
     X. Tour of Perea and Judea, 10:1-52
          Third announcement of Passion, (10:33, 34)
     XI. Ministry in Jerusalem, 11:1—13:37
     XII. The Passion and Resurrection, 14:1—16:20

The Gospel of Luke

SUGGESTED READING   Luke 1—4, 15, 18, 21, 24

AUTHOR   According to the New Testament, Luke was a physician (Col.
                4:14), a companion of Paul (Phile. 24) and the writer of a
two-volume history of the life of Christ and the early Church (Luke, Acts).
His Gospel has long been the favorite of Christian and non-Christian readers
alike because of its sublime presentation of a spotless life. Luke, as Mark,
was not among the original disciples of Christ.

PURPOSE
AND CONTENT Luke addressed his Gospel primarily to Greek (or non-Jewish) readers and presented Jesus as the Son of Man, the ideal human being. As the Greeks had long sought after the "perfect man," Luke's work was designed to fulfill that quest. Some of the most important passages are the account of the birth of Christ (1:26-38; 2:8-20); the testimony of God to His Son (3:21, 22); the announcement of Jesus as the anointed One (4:16-24); the mission of the Son of Man (19:10). Together with these passages should be considered Luke's emphasis on the prayers of Jesus; His matchless parables (especially 10:30-37; 15:1-32; 18:9-14); the human interest features (especially 10:38-42; 19:1-10; 24:13-35) where the Lord deals graciously yet firmly with interesting people; and the prominence of the Holy Spirit in the life of Christ (1:35; 3:22; 4:1, 18; 10:21, asv).

A further illustration of the outreach of this book is the repetition of phrases having relation to humanity. From first to last, Luke shows that the Gospel (God's good news) is meant for all men. See especially 2:10, 14, 31, 32; 3:6; 9:56; 10:33; 17:16; 19:10; 24:47.

OUTLINE The outline is based upon this concept of Christ as "the Son of Man." Luke portrays Him as carrying on a full ministry among the peoples of Palestine with a view to the extension of that ministry to the regions beyond (24:47; cf. Acts 1:8).

    I. Prologue: The Purpose Stated, 1:1-4
    II. The Preparation of the Son of Man, 1:5—4:13
    III. The Galilean Ministry of the Son of Man, 4:14—9:50
    IV. The Perean Ministry of the Son of Man, 9:51—18:30
    V. The Jerusalem Ministry of the Son of Man, 18:31—21:38
    VI. The Passion Ministry of the Son of Man, 22:1—23:56
    VII. The Resurrection Ministry of the Son of Man, 24:1-53

CHARACTERISTICS
COMMON TO
THE GOSPELS While each Gospel has its distinctive emphasis, a number of great events or areas are common to them all. This fact has made these among the best known teachings and events of Christ's ministry.

The Announcement of the Saviour by John the Baptist.
    (Matt. 3; Mark 1; Luke 3.)
The Baptism of the Saviour.
    (Matt. 3; Mark 1; Luke 3.)
The Temptation of the Saviour.
    (Matt. 4; Mark 1; Luke 4.)
The Teachings and Miracles of the Saviour.
    (The major portion of each Gospel.)
The Transfiguration of the Saviour.
    (Matt. 17; Mark 9; Luke 9.)

The Trial, Death, and Burial of the Saviour.
(Matt. 26, 27; Mark 14, 15; Luke 22, 23.)
The Resurrection of the Saviour.
(Matt. 28; Mark 16; Luke 24.)

OTHER SPECIAL FEATURES   In addition, the narrative of His birth and certain events in His life are given in detail.

Unusual nature of Christ's birth

Emphasis is placed upon the unusual nature of His birth: it was prophesied in the Old Testament, announced by an angel to Joseph and Mary, and brought about by the operation of the Holy Spirit (Matt. 1, 2; Luke 1, 2).

The parables of Christ

The teachings and miracles of Christ occupy the major portion of the Gospel records. Distinctive in His teachings was the frequent use of parables. A parable is a story or situation in the human realm which is employed as a means of illustrating or defending some spiritual principle. In these three Gospels at least thirty separate parables are found, plus many other short, axiomatic statements which are parabolic in nature. Among the most notable of these are the parables of the kingdom in Matthew 13 and the parables of the lost things in Luke 15.

The Kingdom

One of the most important areas of our Lord's teaching was concerned with the kingdom. The two expressions, "the kingdom of heaven" and "the kingdom of God" occur often, although the former is limited to Matthew. God's kingdom is essentially "His rule over His creation." It is first of all, a spiritual reality. "The kingdom of God cometh not with observation . . . for lo, the kingdom of God is within you" (Luke 17:20, 21). The kingdom is in the hearts of believers. But then, it is also a visible reality. The Son of Man "shall come in his glory . . . and before him shall be gathered all the nations" (Matt. 25:31, 32). At this time He shall appear and rule over the earth, a theme so prevalent in the prophets (cf. Isa. 11:1-10; Zech. 13:1-6; Mal. 4:1-3). When the kingdom was announced by John the Baptist (Matt. 3:1-3) and by the Lord Jesus. (Mark 1:14, 15), the spiritual aspect was prominent. In the coming of "the Day of the Lord" at the close of this age, the visible aspect will be evidenced. Thus God's program will be fulfilled, all things will be summed up in Christ and ultimately God will be all in all.

The miracles

Alongside His teachings, the miracles of Christ formed an important part of His ministry. They were both evidences of His Messiahship and occasions for bringing needy people to a realization of a greater need than physical necessities—that of spiritual need. In proportion to its length, more miracles are found in Mark than in Matthew and Luke—at least twenty individual situations. This is quite in keeping with Mark, the Gospel of the busy Servant. When the Lord formally announced Himself as God's Anointed at the outset of His public ministry (Luke 4:16-21), He included these two aspects of His commission: the proclamation of the Gospel and the working of miracles. When He had thus announced Himself, He added, "Today hath this scripture been fulfilled in your ears." Both His words and His works were means of revealing God to men. This was the function of the Son (Matt. 11:27).

Suggested Questions and Discussions

1. What is meant by the "Synoptic Gospels"?
2. To whom was each of the Synoptic Gospels written and for what purpose?
3. Summarize the distinctive content of each book.
4. Give at least one important biographical fact about each of the writers of these three Gospels. Illustrate by a Scripture reference for each.
5. Discuss the unique position of the book of Matthew as linking the Old and New Testaments.
6. State the five major discourses of Christ in the book of Matthew.
7. How is the activity of Christ made prominent in Mark?
8. In Luke's Gospel, what are some of the ways in which Jesus is portrayed as the Son of Man?
9. What common characteristics are found in all three books?
10. What are the distinctive characteristics of each book?

Additional Exploration

1. Prepare your own outline of each Synoptic Gospel.
2. For a fuller comprehension of the Synoptic Gospels, prepare a simply-diagrammed chart showing the important features of each, such as main theme, persons, parables, miracles, and teachings.
3. From your study in project 2, note the progression of opposition against Christ. Where did this opposition begin? Where did it end? What type of people were usually the instigators of opposition? What were the issues?
4. Trace the journeys of Christ as presented in the Synoptic Gospels on the map of Palestine, page 22, or on an outline map drawn by you.
5. Summarize Christ's prophetic teachings presented in His Olivet Discourse.
6. Read the remaining chapters not listed in *Suggested Reading*.

Suggested Resources

COLE, A. *The Gospel According to St. Mark: Tyndale New Testament Commentaries*. Grand Rapids: Eerdmans Publishing Co., 1962.

HUNTER, A. M. *The Parables Then and Now*. Philadelphia: Westminster Press, 1972.

STEWART, J. S. *The Life and Teachings of Jesus Christ*. Nashville: Abingdon, 1978.

TASKER, R. V. G. *The Gospel According to St. Matthew: Tyndale New Testament Commentaries*. Grand Rapids: Eerdmans Publishing Co., 1962.

WILCOCK, M. *Savior of the World: The Message of Luke's Gospel*. Downers Grove, IL: Intervarsity Press, 1979.

PALESTINE
IN THE TIME OF
CHRIST

Sidon

Damascus

Sarepta

△ Mt. Hermon

Tyre

PHOENICIA

Caesarea-Philippi

GALILEE

Ptolemais

Chorazin
Capernaum

Bethsaida

Gergesa

Cana

Magdala

Sea of Galilee

Tiberias

Nazareth

Gadara

Nain

Aenon

Caesarea

Scythopolis

DECAPOLIS

THE GREAT SEA

(Mediterranean)

SAMARIA

Samaria

Sychar

Jordan River

PEREA

Joppa

Arimathea

Ephraim

Jamnia

Emmaus

Jericho

Bethphage

Jerusalem

Bethany

Bethlehem

JUDEA

Gaza

Hebron

DEAD SEA

Beersheba

IDUMEA

0   5 10   25
Scale of Miles

CHAPTER THREE

Gospel of John

SUGGESTED READING   John 1—4, 5, 8, 9, 13—17, 20, 21

AUTHOR   According to the persistent tradition of the Church since the early second century, the fourth Gospel was written by John the Apostle, son of Zebedee and brother of James. As one of the Twelve, he was close to Jesus. He is usually identified with the beloved disciple who appears anonymously a number of times within the pages of this book (13:23; 18:15, 16; 19:26, 27).

PURPOSE AND CONTENT   John clearly states his purpose for writing this Gospel (20:30, 31), placing emphasis upon three important words: *signs, believe,* and *life.* A good understanding of these terms, together with their use in the Gospel, allows the reader to gain a working knowledge of its content.

"Signs"

The word "signs" is John's term for the miracles of Jesus.[1] By it he means to impress the reader with the meaning of the miracle, and especially with the revelation of who Jesus really is. Taken together, the signs are meant to show that Jesus is "the Christ, the Son of God."

Out of the many signs which Jesus did, John has selected seven to demonstrate the nature of Christ. Each of them has a particular message.

1. Water changed into wine—Jesus' power over *quality.*
2. The nobleman's son healed—Jesus' power over *distance.*
3. The impotent man healed—Jesus' power over *time.*
4. The five thousand fed—Jesus' power over *quantity.*
5. Walking on the water—Jesus' power over *natural law.*
6. The blind man healed—Jesus' power over *helplessness.*
7. Lazarus raised from the dead—Jesus' power over *death.*

Of the seven, five are found only in John's Gospel. The feeding of the five thousand is the only miracle recorded by all the writers; the walking on the water appears also in Matthew and Mark.

---

[1] The most common words in the other Gospels are "powers" and "wonders." The former denotes the display of supernatural power in doing the miracle; the latter emphasizes the effect of the miracle upon the people—it left them awestruck.

"Believe"

One of the most frequent words in the book, "believe," appears at least ninety-eight times. It always occurs in the verb form, never the noun form ("believe," never "belief"). This continually gives the impression of action, of something happening. John is teaching the meaning of believing in Jesus not so much by definition as by illustration. The word is used to indicate the response of people to Jesus. If they believed on Him, they became His followers; if they did not believe, they became His opponents. At any rate, once having met Him, they could not remain neutral.

Along with the word "believe," John employs a number of synonyms to make his meaning clear. Some of these are "receive" (1:12), "drink" (4:14), "come" (6:35), "eat" (6:51), "enter" (10:9). All these words, used in the routine of daily life, become full with meaning when applied to the spiritual relationship of men to Christ. Believing on Him is like receiving a gift, drinking refreshing water, entering by a door into a sheepfold. The need is met, the thirst is quenched, the hunger is satiated.

"Life"

This term expresses the result of believing in Him. To receive life is to become a child of God by being born into His family. It is the divine nature imparted to the believer. The Lord Jesus said to the Pharisee, Nicodemus: "Except one be born anew, he cannot see the kingdom of God" (3:3). This life is described as eternal in quality (3:15) and is, therefore, the opposite of the state of spiritual death which means to perish (3:16).

In addition, there will be a manifestation of this gift in the one who receives it. The Holy Spirit, who is the agent of regeneration, will be as rivers of living water flowing from within the one who has drunk of the water of life (7:37-39). Thus the life is imparted to others around the believer, as dry ground is refreshed by a stream.

Thus, John has stated his purpose. In writing the story of Christ, he has sought to bring his readers face to face with this Person who by His words and His works confronts men and women with a great decision. From first to last He is described as deity (1:1; 20:28). Yet He has come in human form (1:14) so that He might give Himself to bring life to those who sit in the shadow of death (12:23, 24). Not only did He die, but He rose again (chap. 20). As the living Lord, He calls forth the devotion and loyalty of His followers (21:15-19).

OUTLINE

    I. Prologue: The Presentation of the Son of God, 1:1-18
   II. The Public Ministry of the Son of God, 1:19—12:50
        A. Confronting individuals, 1:19—4:54
        B. Confronting the multitudes, 5:1—6:71
        C. Conflicting with the multitudes, 7:1—11:53
        D. Climaxing the public ministry, 11:54—12:50

CHRIST'S TEACHINGS   Having gained a general idea of what John has done in writing his Gospel, let us consider the teachings of the Lord Jesus. What does He teach and how does He impart these truths to the people?

The relationship between the signs and His teaching

The signs were occasions for Jesus' teaching, so that one may expect to find this order followed in the book.

In chapter 5, Jesus healed the infirmed man beside the pool of Bethesda in Jerusalem. Following the sign, the Jews challenged His right to do such a thing on the Sabbath Day (5:16). This called forth His claims of equality with God in *nature* (5:17, 18), in *power* (5:21), and in *authority* (5:26, 27). To substantiate these claims, He called upon certain witnesses including John the Baptist (5:33), His own works (5:36), the Father (5:37), the Scriptures (5:39), and Moses (5:46).

In chapter 6, Jesus was faced with the task of feeding more than five thousand hungry people. After His disciple Philip had failed to provide a solution to the problem, Andrew brought a boy to Jesus with his lunch of five barley loaves and two fishes (6:9). Using these, He fed the people and thus met their physical need (6:12). When the crowd returned the following day, obviously looking for another "free meal," the Lord admonished them to "stop working for the food which perisheth" (6:27). Then He taught them of their spiritual need and declared, "I am the bread of life" (6:35). A lengthy discourse followed in which He drew a contrast between "the flesh" and "the spirit" (6:63). He uncovered the shortcomings in their understanding of spiritual realities. They held improper *motives* (6:26), coming to Him only for physical bread; they had missed the meaning of the sign. They employed improper *methods* (6:28), failing to do the works of God. They retained an improper *conception* of their religious heritage (6:30, 31), placing Christ on the same level as Moses. And they evidenced an improper *desire* in asking for "this bread" (6:34), for when He explained what it meant "to eat the living bread," they murmured (6:41), strove one with another (6:52) and, finally, many of those who followed Him turned away (6:66).

In addition to these two outstanding examples, the sign of chapter 9 is an admirable illustration of His claim, "I am the light of the world" (8:12; 9:5), and the sign of chapter 11 makes clear His claim, "I am the resurrection and the life" (11:25).

The seven "I am's"

The Lord Jesus makes claims for Himself by means of the "I am" phrases in this Gospel. Although some of these have been referred to in passing, the complete list should be carefully observed by the reader.

1. "I am the bread of life" (6:35).
2. "I am the light of the world" (8:12; 9:5).
3. "I am the door" (10:7, 9).
4. "I am the good shepherd" (10:11).
5. "I am the resurrection and the life" (11:25).
6. "I am the way, the truth, and the life" (14:6).
7. "I am the true vine" (15:1).

Aside from the graphic figures which Christ employed in thus describing Himself, the striking thing about these claims is the exclusive nature of them. First, the original form "I am" is an emphatic grammatical construction. Then, He is "the only way"; no one comes to God except by Him (14:6). He is the "true vine," that is the original, as contrasted with any copy or imitation. The alternative to eating "the bread of life" is death; if one refuses "the light," he remains in darkness. Along with these expressions, the Lord states to the Jews, "Verily, verily, I say unto you, before Abraham was born, I am" (8:58). He thus took upon Himself the title of deity from their Old Testament Scriptures, for this was the title by which God revealed Himself to Moses (Exod. 3:14).

The personal interview

Of great importance in communicating his message is John's use of the personal interviews. Again and again, people are brought into contact with Jesus. They are never the same again. Either they believe and follow Him, or they turn away in unbelief. While there are many such situations in the book, the main examples include:

1. Andrew (1:35-42; 6:8, 9; 12:20-22).

Though Andrew was not so well-known as his brother Simon Peter, he possessed noteworthy qualities. Andrew, having believed in Jesus for himself, became a personal worker. He is always seen bringing someone else to Jesus. First, his brother, Simon; then a lad; then the Greek visitors in Jerusalem.

2. Simon Peter (1:42; 6:68, 69; 13:36-38; 18:15-18, 25-27; 21:15-22).

When Peter met Jesus, the prophecy of his new name (meaning a change in character) was given. He was "unstable" (Simon); he would become "firm" (Cephas, "a rock"). Along with this he was ready to confess his faith in Jesus as "the Holy One of God." Although he was overconfident, leading to his temporary denial of his Lord, yet he was graciously restored and recommissioned to follow Christ anew and feed His sheep.

3. Nicodemus (3:1 ff.; 7:50, 51; 19:39-42).

Although Nicodemus was a man thoroughly trained in the Old Testament truths, he had not experienced the new birth; he did not have a realization of the Messiahship of Jesus. The Lord showed him how He fulfilled the Old Testament type of the serpent in the wilderness, and that as God's Son He was sent to be the Saviour of all who would believe in Him. That Nicodemus came to true belief seems to be indicated by the incidents which follow in the book.

Using the same approach, the following additional important people in John's Gospel are worthy of study:

4. Philip (1:43-46; 6:5-7; 14:8-12).

5. The woman of Samaria (4:1-42).

6. The blind man (chap. 9).

7. Martha and Mary (11:1-46).

8. Thomas (11:16; 14:5-7; 20:24-28).

In him is seen the culmination of belief in John's Gospel with his confession of the deity of Christ—"my Lord and my God."

9. Pilate (18:28—19:16).

He is the outstanding example of unbelief in the Gospel, along with Judas Iscariot (6:70, 71; 13:21-30; 18:1-5).

Upper Room Discourse

Attention should be given to that unique discourse of the Gospel found in chapters 13—16, commonly called the Upper Room Discourse. Bishop B. F. Westcott calculated that 92 percent of the material in John was unique and that, consequently, only 8 percent was material held in common with the Synoptic Gospels. Of John's unique material, this section is the most outstanding unit in the book. After His public ministry was concluded (at the end of chap. 12), Jesus met privately with His disciples and told them of two important things which were soon to happen. First, His departure was near. He was going away; they could not come with Him at this point. Eventually, however, He would return to receive them into the Father's house. Second, the Holy Spirit would be sent to take His place. He would not leave the disciples alone (literally, "orphans," 14:18). He would send "another Comforter," One "just like Himself." The Holy Spirit would indwell them (14:17), teach them (14:26), empower them to witness (15:26, 27), and guide them into all the truth (16:13).

PROLOGUE AND EPILOGUE Finally, notice the opening and closing sections of the book, the Prologue (1:1-18) and the Epilogue (21:1-25). The former contains the message of the entire Gospel. John introduces (1) the chief character of the book—"the Word."

He is God, the Creator, the Giver of Life, the One manifest in flesh, and the Revealer of the Father. (2) The chief vocabulary terms of the book— "life," "light," "darkness," "witness," "believe," "truth." (3) The chief plot of the book—"conflict." Notice the words used to illustrate spiritual conflict: light vs. darkness; received him not vs. received him; physical birth vs. spiritual birth; law vs. grace and truth. This conflict continues throughout the book until it culminates in the cross and the resurrection.

The epilogue furnishes an appropriate climax to the Gospel. It teaches the logical result of believing in Jesus. If one truly believes, he will *follow* Jesus and thus give expression to his faith in service (21:19). Peter learned that believing in Jesus did not only eventuate in the spoken word of confession, but in the life of dedicated service.

Suggested Questions and Discussions

1. State John's purpose in writing the Gospel.
2. Define and show the importance of each of the three words: *signs, believe, life.*
3. What is the relationship generally observed between the signs and the teachings of Christ as presented in the Gospel of John?
4. What is the striking feature about the *I am* claims of Christ? Illustrate this from Scripture.
5. In your own words, summarize the personal interviews that Andrew, the blind man, and Thomas had with Christ.
6. What two important messages were communicated in the Upper Room Discourse?
7. What is the contribution of the Prologue to the message of John?
8. What does the Epilogue of the book emphasize?

Additional Exploration

1. Trace the Scriptures in John that reveal Christ's deity. Keep for future use.
2. List and summarize all the passages in John which refer to the Holy Spirit.
3. In John's Gospel, list Christ's various titles and their significance.
   Compare these with your findings concerning the Holy Spirit in project 2.
4. To help you master the Gospel of John, prepare your own comprehensive outline.
5. Using the chart idea suggested in chapter II, project 2, trace events in Christ's life recorded in John's Gospel. What is the significance of John's writing of events which are not included in the other three Gospels?

Suggested Resources

BROWN, R. E. *The Gospel According to John: The Anchor Bible.* 2 vol. Garden City, NY: Doubleday, 1966, 1970.

HENDRICKSEN, WILLIAM. *A Commentary on the Gospel of John.* New Testament Commentary. 2 vols. Grand Rapids: Eerdmans Publishing Co., 1961.

HUNTER, A. M. *Gospel According to John.* New York: Cambridge Univ. Press, 1965.

MORRIS, L. *Gospel of John: New International Commentary on the New Testament.* Grand Rapids: Eerdmans Publishing Co., 1970.

TENNEY, MERRILL C. *John: The Gospel of Belief.* Grand Rapids: Eerdmans Publishing Co., 1948.

CHAPTER FOUR

Book of Acts

SUGGESTED READING   Acts 1—3, 6—9, 13—21, 27, 28

This is the second volume of Luke's history of Christianity. Without the book of Acts, many details of the life of the early Church would be missing. Of the first thirty years we would know only what could be pieced together from the New Testament Epistles.

From the book itself we discover that Luke the author was a companion of Paul and an eyewitness to many of the events about which he writes. This evidence appears in the so-called "we-sections" of the text, that is, places where Luke includes himself in the story by the use of the first person plural pronoun (16:10-17; 20:5—21:18; 27:1—28:16). Besides Luke's firsthand experiences, he also had occasions for personal interviews. Paul was able to tell him of his Gentile ministry. From leaders at Jerusalem he could gather valuable sources concerning the Jerusalem Church. His contact with Philip in Caesarea gave access to data of Philip's Samaritan ministry.

PURPOSE   Why did Luke write the book of Acts? What were the chief motives which lay behind his work? Consider the following:

The historical motive

This is the most obvious one, of course. Acts is a continuation of the narrative begun in the Gospel of Luke (Luke 1:1-4; cf. Acts 1:1-5). The books are addressed to the same individual, Theophilus. They are linked together by the phrase, "the former treatise." One concerns what "Jesus began both to do and teach," while the other records the continuation of that ministry by "the apostles whom he had chosen."

Again, compare Luke 24:44-53 with Acts 1:6-11. Both passages speak of the coming of the Holy Spirit, of the disciples as witnesses, and of the ascension of the Lord Jesus into heaven.

Luke, therefore, gives his readers the history of the first 60 or 65 years of Christianity. About 30 years would be included in each of his two works. It is the story of the good news of salvation, beginning in a manger in Bethlehem and extending to the very hub of the Empire, Rome itself (cf. Phil. 4:22). The narrative opens with the witness of the shepherds in the fields of Judea and terminates with the salutations of saints in Caesar's household.

The doctrinal motive

As in his Gospel, so here also, Luke's chief doctrinal emphasis is upon the person and work of the Holy Spirit. In fact, the explicit references to the Spirit in Acts occur with great frequency (Acts 1—11; 13, 15, 16, 19, 20, 21, and 28). The Lord Jesus, in His last recorded utterance prior to the Ascension, promised the disciples that "ye shall receive power, when the Holy Spirit is come upon you," and the fulfillment of that promise is clearly seen in the Acts. He was the motivating power in their witness and work for Christ. He filled them again and again (cf. 2:4; 4:8, 31; 6:5; 7:55; 9:18; 11:24, 13:9). In situations where discipline (5:3, 4), wisdom (6:3), or guidance (16:6, 7) was required, the Holy Spirit operated in the believers. By His coming, differing groups were united into that one great company, the Church (the Jews, chap. 2; the Samaritans, chap. 8; the Gentiles, chap. 10; some disciples of John, chap. 19).

The apologetic motive

In one sense, the book of Acts is simply a defense of Christianity. That believers need to defend (I Pet. 3:15; Phil. 1:18) and contend for the faith is clear (Jude 3). Luke shows to the world that in the first generation, the Church was never the object of official persecution at the hands of the Roman government. The Jews, often; but the Romans, never. This is a remarkable record which, at that particular time when Paul had appealed to Caesar for a fair trial, needed to be clearly stated.

In each of the contacts between the apostles and officials of the Roman government, they were either accepted or ignored but never persecuted. A number of these situations are recorded by Luke:

1. Paul and Barnabas before Sergius Paulus, the proconsul at Cyrus; he "believed" (Acts 13).
2. Paul and Silas in Philippi (Acts 16). The Roman jailer was saved, and the magistrates of this Roman colony apologized for the unjust treatment accorded the missionaries because of the false charges of the Jews.
3. Paul before Gallio, the proconsul of Achaia; he "cared for none of these things" (i.e., problems of Jewish law, Acts 18). Gallio was indifferent.
4. Paul in Ephesus (Acts 19). The Asiarchs (v. 31) were friends of Paul; the town clerk restored order, thereby rescuing the missionaries from possible violence.
5. Paul safeguarded by Claudius Lysias, the Roman captain of the castle Antonia in Jerusalem (Acts 21, 22).
6. Paul before Felix in Caesarea; he often called for and listened to Paul speak (Acts 24).
7. Paul before Festus in Caesarea; he considered Paul innocent of the charges against him by the Jews (Acts 25).

When persecution against the apostles and the Church does appear in Acts, it is at the hands of the Jews—either the Sanhedrin or groups such as those who follow Paul in his journeys (cf. chaps. 4, 5, 7, 8, 16, 17, 18) and the silversmiths of Ephesus (Acts 19).

The biographical motive

Of the many interesting and important persons who appear in Acts, Peter and Paul are those to whom Luke gives a place of prominence. His record is concentrated largely upon their activities. Peter occupies the major portion of chapters 1—12; Paul of chapters 13—28.

It might be said that the first generation of the Church was the story of these two. The Jerusalem church was led by Peter for the first few years of its existence. Even the early probings into surrounding areas, such as Samaria (chap. 8) and Caesarea (chap. 10) were to one degree or another the work of Peter. The ministry of the Gospel in the Gentile lands, from Syria to Rome itself, was mainly carried on by Paul. In the great provinces of Galatia, Macedonia, Achaia, and Asia, he founded churches and established them in their newfound faith.

Working alongside Peter and Paul were a number of other notable individuals: Stephen (chaps. 6, 7); Philip the evangelist (chap. 8); Barnabas (chaps. 4, 9, 11, 13—15); John Mark (chaps. 12, 13, 15); Silas (chaps. 15, 16, 17); Timothy (chaps. 16, 17); Aquila and Priscilla (chap. 18); Apollos (chaps. 18, 19). Some of these and others as well, also appear in Paul's epistles, where they are described as his fellow-workers.

In giving this record, then, Luke has made it clear what people were actively responsible for the growth and expansion of the Church. Thus the epistles are illuminated for us by his biographical portraits.

OUTLINE The key verse of Acts (1:8) provides a basis for the outline of the book. As the Lord Jesus spoke of the future ministry to be accomplished by His followers, consequent upon the coming of the Holy Spirit, He stressed two things: (1) *persons,* and (2) *places.* "Ye shall be my witnesses"—that is the personnel of the mission. "In Jerusalem, and in all Judea and Samaria, and unto the uttermost part of the earth"—that is the geography of the mission. The main divisions of the outline reveal the primary locations; the subpoints indicate the chief persons in each place.

    I. Introduction: The Apostolic Commission Given, 1:1-11

   II. The Gospel in Jerusalem: Origins, 1:12—8:3
      A. The ministry of Peter, 1:12—5:42
      B. The ministry of Stephen, 6:1—8:3

  III. The Gospel in Samaria and Judea: Transition, 8:4—11:18
      A. The ministry of Philip, 8:4-40
      B. The ministry of Saul begun, 9:1-31
      C. The ministry of Peter concluded, 9:32—11:18

  IV. The Gospel in the Uttermost Part: Expansion, 11:19—21:14

THE GOSPEL IN JERUSALEM In the first section of Acts, it is Peter who plays a part in a variety of situations. He assumes the leadership after the ascension of the Lord and is instrumental in bringing about the election of Matthias to replace Judas Iscariot, a suicide. Peter preaches the notable sermon on the Day of Pentecost resulting in the salvation of three thousand persons. He and John heal the lame man at the Temple gate and subsequently defend their act and preaching before the Jewish Sanhedrin. It is Peter who condemns Ananias and Sapphira for their plot to deceive the Church and leads the congregation in the choice of the seven to supervise the distribution of goods to the widows.

One thing which is outstanding throughout this narrative is the spirit of unity which prevailed among the Christians. Notice carefully the references which illustrate this condition, especially the first prayer meeting (1:14); the preparation for Pentecost (2:1); the sharing of goods and consistent witness (2:43-47; 4:23-31), the prayer for boldness (4:23-31), the daily ministry of the Word (5:41, 42).

Near the end of the opening unit, Stephen is featured as a mighty and fearless defender of the faith. While he loses his life, becoming the first martyr of the Church, his influence endures. This is especially important in the case of one of the spectators at his martyrdom, a young man named Saul (7:58), who later is brought to Christ and becomes Paul the Apostle. At this point, however, he sets out to persecute the believers and forces them all, except the apostles, to flee from Jerusalem.

THE GOSPEL IN JUDEA AND SAMARIA The second major section of the book concerns the work of the Church in the regions of Judea and Samaria, just to the north of Jerusalem. Philip the evangelist, one of the seven chosen in chapter 6, went to Samaria and the result was most gratifying. Many believed his message concerning Christ. When the church in Jerusalem heard the news, Peter and John were sent to confirm them in their newfound faith (Acts 8:15-17). Philip departed to the south, near Gaza, and led the Ethiopian treasurer to Christ, Peter went on toward the seacoast, eventually coming to the home of Cornelius, the Roman centurion in Caesarea, and had the joy of witnessing the salvation of that man and those of his household. With the reception of the Holy Spirit, these Gentile believers were recognized as sharing in the fellowship of the Church with the Jews (chap. 2) and the Samaritans (chap. 8).

During this period of the history the conversion of Saul occurs (chap. 9). That Luke attaches great importance to this event is evidenced by his three long accounts of the incident (cf. chaps. 9, 22, 26). With this, the chief persecutor of the Church becomes changed into her most prominent defender and preacher.

THE GOSPEL TO THE UTTERMOST The third and most lengthy unit of Acts is mainly the record of the development and expansion of the Gentile ministry led by Paul and his fellow workers.[1] Going back to the record of Saul's persecution of the Church in Jerusalem (cf. 11:19 with 8:1-4), Luke first traces the progress of the Gospel from the home base to the Syrian city of Antioch. Here the narrative resumes with the dispatching of Barnabas to establish the new believers in that important city. Antioch, ranked as the third city of the Empire (after Rome and Alexandria), became the home base for missionary work among the Gentiles. After Barnabas went to Tarsus and brought Saul back with him, the two worked together in the Church until it was thriving. It was here they were first called Christians (11:26). Then, following a brief trip to Jerusalem to deliver needed goods to the famine-stricken Christians in Jerusalem, these two men were called by the Holy Spirit to a new and larger work—and the missionary journeys of Paul began.

As the accompanying chart will make clear the particulars of the missionary ventures, it will be necessary here only to emphasize some of the significant highlights of this part of the narrative.

THE JOURNEYS OF PAUL The initial journey was concentrated primarily in the province of Galatia (chaps. 13—15); the second in the provinces of Macedonia and Achaia (chaps. 16—18); the third in the province of Asia (chaps. 19—20).[2] In these places, Paul spent most of his time in population centers—cities like Antioch of Pisidia, Philippi, Thessalonica, Corinth, and Ephesus. Once the evangelization of these cities had been completed, the Gospel radiated to the surrounding country (cf. I Thess. 1:8).

Paul found himself in a variety of situations and audiences. On occasion the missionary was in the Jewish synagogue (as in Pisidian Antioch, Thessa-

---

Chap. 12 is a glimpse into the persecution of some of the church leaders. James, the brother of John, was killed and Peter was imprisoned. When released, he left the city and James, the brother of Christ, became the leader of the Jerusalem church

[2]Between the record of the first and second journeys is the narrative of the Jerusalem Council, occasioned by the teaching of certain men that the Gentiles must observe the Jewish law (cf. 15:19-21, 28, 29)

The Missionary Journeys of Paul

Refs.	Places Visited	Personnel	Main Events	Main Results
I Acts 13:4 – 14:28	Departure from Antioch (Syria) Seleucia Cyprus: Salamis Paphos Pamphylia: Perga Galatia: Antioch Iconium Lystra Derbe Return to Antioch (Syria)	Paul Barnabas John Mark	Contest with Elymas at Paphos Sermon in synagogue at Antioch (Pisidia) Paul and Barnabas worshiped at Lystra Paul preaches, then is stoned at Lystra	Conversion of Sergius Paulus at Paphos Conversions and riot at Antioch (Pisidia) Churches founded and established in all Galatian cities; elders appointed Report of journey to the Church in Antioch (Syria)
II Acts 15:36 – 18:22	Departure from Antioch (Syria) Syria and Cilicia Galatia: Derbe and Lystra Troas Macedonia: Philippi Thessalonica Berea Achaia: Athens Corinth Asia: Ephesus Caesarea Return to Antioch (Syria)	Paul Silas Timothy (Luke)	Timothy added to party at Lystra Vision at Troas; Luke added to party Preaching and imprisonment at Philippi Preaching and persecution at Thessalonica Preaching at Berea Sermon on Mars' Hill in Athens Eighteen-month stay at Corinth, teaching, trial before Gallio Short stay at Ephesus, preaching	Conversion of Lydia and the jailer at Philippi. Church founded Church founded at Thessalonica Conversion of Dionysius and Damaris at Athens Church founded at Corinth
III Acts 18:23 – 21:14	Departure from Antioch (Syria) Galatia and Phrygia Asia: Ephesus Macedonia Greece Macedonian cities Troas Asia: Melitus Syria: Tyre Ptolemais Caesarea Jerusalem	Paul Silas Timothy (Luke) Gaius Aristarchus Sopater Secundus Tychicus Trophimus	Teaching ministry in Ephesus (2-3 years) Riot of the Ephesian silversmiths Preaching at Troas Eutychus restored to life Farewell to the Ephesian elders at Miletus Warning to Paul at Tyre regarding Jerusalem Warning to Paul at Caesarea by Agabus regarding Jerusalem	Church established at Ephesus; center of evangelization of Asia Instruction to the Ephesian elders regarding official duties

THE
FIRST AND SECOND
MISSIONARY JOURNEYS
— OF —
ST. PAUL

First Journey ━━━━━━
Second Journey ••••••••

BLACK SEA

MOESIA
THRACIA
MACEDONIA
ILLYRICUM
ADRIATIC SEA
ITALY
SICILY

PONTUS
GALATIA
CAPPADOCIA
BITHYNIA
Ancyra

SAMOTHRACIA
Neapolis
Philippi
Amphipolis
Apollonia
Thessalonica
Berea
ACHAIA

PHRYGIA
MYSIA
Troas
Assos
ASIA
Ephesus
CARIA

AEGEAN SEA
Athens
Corinth
GREECE

CRETE

MEDITERRANEAN SEA

LIBYA
EGYPT
Alexandria

Iconium
Lystra
Derbe
PISIDIA
Antioch
Tarsus
CILICIA
LYCIA
PAMPHYLIA
Perga
Attalia

Seleucia
Antioch
SYRIA
Damascus
Salamis
CYPRUS
Paphos

Sidon
Tyre
Ptolemais
Caesaria
Samaria
Joppa
Jerusalem
Gaza

DEAD SEA

THE
— THIRD —
MISSIONARY JOURNEY
— OF —
ST. PAUL
AND HIS VOYAGE TO ROME

Third Journey — — —
Voyage to Rome ▪▪▪▪▪▪▪▪

lonica, Athens, Corinth, and Ephesus); or before the leaders of the city (as in Athens); or in prison (as in Philippi). When preaching to a Jewish audience, Paul used the Old Testament Scriptures as a basis for his message (as in Antioch and Thessalonica); whereas in addressing pagan, or at least non-Jewish groups, he generally began with their natural surroundings(as in Lystra and Athens). His usual approach was to preach first to the Jews of the region, if they were to be found; then to the Gentiles.

Paul's ministry in these areas, covering a period of about ten years, resulted in the establishment of a chain of churches all along the Mediterranean shores. As he wrote to the Roman Christians, he recalled that "from Jerusalem, and round about even unto Illyricum, I have fully preached the gospel of Christ" (Rom. 15:19). This period of his labors was terminated with the final visit to Jerusalem which resulted in his arrest (on a false charge by some Asian Jews) and his consequent imprisonments, both in Caesarea and Rome.

The final section of Acts is the record of Paul's experiences while a prisoner. He makes his defense before a Jewish mob and the Jewish leaders in Jerusalem (chaps. 22, 23), before Felix, Festus, and Herod Agrippa II in Caesarea (chaps. 24—26) and finally is taken to Rome, amid many harrowing experiences, including shipwreck (chaps. 27, 28). Here, in his own rented house, though constantly chained to a guard, he is free to carry on his preaching and teaching. No wonder "they of Caesar's household" heard and received the good news of salvation.

RELATIONSHIP OF ACTS TO THE GOSPELS AND THE EPISTLES   Before closing this study, the character of Acts as a central book in the New Testament should be noted. It is the bridge between the Gospels and the Epistles and therefore has close ties to each of these writings.

First, it continues and, in one sense, completes the narrative begun in the Gospels. The earthly life of Christ is followed by the ministry of His apostles.

Second, it shows the fulfillment of our Lord's prophecy of the Church (Matt. 16:18) and prepares the way for the expounding of this subject in the Epistles. Many questions are thus answered regarding the circumstances of its beginning, the early leaders, and its growth into a universal fellowship.

Third, it gives the background for several of Paul's epistles, relating the details concerning the founding of the churches to which the letters were subsequently written.

Background for Galatians—Antioch, Iconium, Lystra, and Derbe (Acts 13:14—14:28).

Background for Philippians—Philippi (Acts 16:11-40).

Background for I and II Thessalonians—Thessalonica (Acts 17:1-9).

Background for I and II Corinthians—Corinth (Acts 18:1-16).

Background for Ephesians—Ephesus (Acts 19:1-41; 20:17:35; cf. also I and II Tim.).

By reading these chapters before reading the respective epistles, light is cast on the nature of the city, the people, and the problems faced by Paul.

Fourth, it illustrates in the active life of the Church many of the principles enunciated in the Epistles. Such matters as organization, discipline, witnessing, evangelism, and teaching are clearly mirrored in the narratives of Acts. Especially prominent is the stress upon the necessity of the work of the Holy Spirit. The early Church not only taught this truth but experienced it as well.

Suggested Questions and Discussions

1. List Luke's four motives for writing Acts. Show how each is reflected within the narrative.
2. What is the key verse of Acts? In what ways does it provide the framework for the rest of the book?
3. Summarize in your own words the account of the proclamation of the Gospel in Jerusalem (Acts 1:12—8:3).
4. Summarize in your words the account of the proclamation of the Gospel in Judea and Samaria (Acts 8:4—11:18).
5. In what provinces were each of Paul's three missionary journeys centered?
6. Name the two most prominent individuals associated with Paul in each of the three missionary journeys.
7. What is the relationship of the book of Acts to the Gospels and the Epistles?

Additional Exploration

1. List some of the problems of the early Church. How were these solved? Relate these to the present-day Church.
2. Study carefully the chart and maps of Paul's missionary journeys. Taking each journey separately, be able to trace in order the main places and events.
3. Appraise the various ministries of some of the outstanding personalities in the book of Acts—especially Stephen, Peter, Philip, and Paul. Observe the influence of the Holy Spirit in each life. Compare your observations with your study of the various aspects of Christ's life.
4. List ways that your church can enrich and expand its ministry in various fields of Christian activity. Use the book of Acts as your guidebook.
5. For better appreciation of New Testament faith and practice, prepare your own comprehensive outline of the book of Acts.

Suggested Resources

BRUCE, F. F. *Book of the Acts: New International Commentary on the New Testament.* Grand Rapids: Eerdmans Publishing Co., 1954.

HARRISON, E. F. *Acts: The Expanding Church.* Chicago: Moody Press, 1976.

RAMSEY, SIR WILLIAM M. *St. Paul the Traveller and the Roman Citizen.* Grand Rapids: Baker Book House, 1982.

VAUGHAN, C. *Acts: A Study Guide Commentary.* Grand Rapids: Zondervan Pub. House, 1974.

CHAPTER FIVE

Pauline Epistles

I and II Thessalonians

As a letter writer and as a man, Paul has no superior in the history of the Church. His life story is one of the most amazing in the history of mankind, and people of all ages since the beginning of the Christian era have, in one way or another, been indebted to him. Before giving attention to the written legacy which he has left, the main details of his life must be considered.

The best insights into his life come from his own pen and are to be found in several of the epistles, particularly Philippians, Galatians, and the Corinthian letters. In addition, the three accounts of Paul's conversion experience and the record of his activities and witness recorded in the book of Acts give valuable information.

BACKGROUND OF PAUL Paul was first and foremost a Jew. This is the main factor in understanding his character and activities. He was born of Jewish parentage in the city of Tarsus, in the province of Cilicia, and was thus known for many years as Saul of Tarsus. According to his own testimony he was a Pharisee, as his father had been before him (Acts 23:6), spoke the Aramaic tongue ("a Hebrew of the Hebrews"), and was taught the trade of tentmaking in his youth (Acts 18:3). Further, he was of the tribe of Benjamin (Phil. 3:5). Historically, the Benjamites were fighters, and Paul seems to give evidence of an abundance of zeal in all his endeavors, especially in the persecution of the Church (Gal. 1:13). At an early age he went to Jerusalem, and according to his recorded testimony in Acts, studied under the noted Rabban Gamaliel I, leading teacher of the School of Hillel (22:3).[1] From his own words in Galatians, we learn that Saul had "advanced in the Jew's religion" beyond many of his fellows, "being more exceedingly zealous for the traditions of my fathers" (1:14).

The beginning of Saul's furious campaign to exterminate the Church coincided with the murder of Stephen (Acts 7:58—8:3). Not only did he persecute "both men and women" in Jerusalem, but, with letters of arrest from the high priest (Joseph Caiaphas), he went to other cities as well to

---

[1] The two prominent Rabbinical schools dated back to Hillel and Shammai. Hillel allowed his students greater freedom in their education, even to the reading of Greek writers.

carry on his work (Acts 26:10, 11). It was on one such mission that Saul of Tarsus met Jesus and was dramatically converted.

Saul was a Greek by culture. Not only was he reared in one of the leading centers of Greek learning, but he shows an acquaintance with the Greek mind. As an intelligent scholar, Saul knew many of the commonly used sayings taken from classical and contemporary writers (Acts 17:28; Titus 1:12). Too, he had a "world outlook." Unlike the man of provincial demeanor, Paul could write, "I am become all things to all men, that I may by all means save some" (I Cor. 9:22). Thus, by his background, he was suited to stand before the Gentiles proclaiming Jesus' Name.

Further, Saul was a Roman citizen. When questioned about his status by the Roman captain in Jerusalem who had informed his prisoner that he had purchased the coveted citizenship with "a great sum," Paul replied with pride, "But I am *a Roman* born" (Acts 22:28). He had appealed to his citizenship rights earlier in Philippi to gain proper respect from the local magistrates (Acts 16:37-39). This status allowed a number of valuable rights such as the right of proper trial before condemnation and punishment, the right of appeal to Caesar for justice (cf. Acts 25:11, 12) and, in event of the death penalty, execution by decapitation rather than crucifixion.

CONVERSION   One day, with suddenness, it happened! The thing that
OF PAUL   Saul, at least, never could have imagined would happen
to him occurred with revolutionary effects. He had denied the Christian claim that Jesus was the Messiah, the Son of God. Further, he did not believe that He had risen from the dead as Stephen had proclaimed when he cried, "Behold, I see the heavens opened, and the Son of man standing on the right hand of God" (Acts 7:56). "Liar!" they cried and stoned him. Saul stood by "consenting unto his death." But when the Lord Jesus spoke to Saul on the day of the great experience outside Damascus, he knew that Stephen had been right and he had been wrong. Jesus was alive after all! And further, he must be the Son of God. Thus, in the synagogues of Damascus, he proclaimed Christ as Saviour.

To explain exactly what happened to Saul is difficult. But there can be little doubt, from Paul's own testimony, that the change in his life was due to a personal encounter with Christ and a new relationship to Him (Gal. 2:20; Phil. 3:7 ff.; II Cor. 5:14-19). While the experience was sudden and dramatic, the effects were enduring. The impact must have necessitated great psychological and intellectual readjustments. This may well account for the period spent in Arabia and Damascus before his first visit to Jerusalem (Gal. 1:16-19). Then he went back to his home territory and for a period of eight to ten years little is known of his activities.[2]

---

[2]Possibly Gal. 1:23 hints at a preaching ministry during these so-called "silent years," but the evidence is scant.

Paul leaves us in no doubt, however, that Christ had both appointed him an apostle and revealed the Gospel to him, so that "he might preach it among the Gentiles." (See esp. Gal. 1:1-20.)

MINISTRY With the invitation of Barnabas to join him at Syrian Antioch
OF PAUL begin the missionary labors of Paul. For the next twenty years
or so he carried on a vast ministry.

Background

Beginning in Antioch (Acts 11:25, 26) he later evangelized the provinces of Galatia, Macedonia, Achaia, and Asia, besides many smaller areas as well. He founded, established, and organized churches in all these areas.

Together with Barnabas, Peter, James, and other leaders of the Church, Paul had a major part in resolving the problem of the basis of Gentile salvation and the matters of fellowship between Jew and Gentile (cf. Acts 15:1-35; Gal. 2:1-10). Paul's wide outlook and genuine concern that the Gospel might reach out to all the world triumphed over the narrower perspective and more limited concern of the Jerusalem apostles. He had truly caught the vision of his Lord that the message should go out to all nations.

His written ministry

At least thirteen samples of his correspondence have been preserved, and he doubtless wrote many others which did not survive.[3] His written ministry shows great diversity and yet the letters may be naturally grouped under four basic headings, each reflecting a common emphasis. An attempt is also made to indicate an approximate chronological sequence, though any sense of finality here is impossible.

1. The Eschatological Letters: I and II Thessalonians.

Date: about A.D. 50-51. These epistles emphasize the doctrine of the last things and are especially concerned with the Second Coming of Christ and the implications of that event in the present life of the believer.

2. The Soteriological Letters: I and II Corinthians, Galatians, and Romans.

Date: about A.D. 55-58.[4] Various aspects of the doctrine of salvation are delineated in this class of letters. The Corinthian Epistles stress the application of salvation to the life of the Church; Romans and Galatians reflect the doctrine of justification and its outward expression in Christian living.

3. The Christological Letters: Colossians, Philemon, Ephesians, and Philippians.

---

[3] I Cor. 5:9 indicates at least one such instance.

[4] Although Gal. belongs in this group on the basis of its subject matter, it may well have been written earlier. Some place it as early as 48/49, others about 52/53. The date, however, does not affect its teaching.

Date: about A.D. 60-62. Often called the Prison Epistles, as they were written (according to tradition as well as internal evidences) from Paul's prison in Rome (Acts 28:30, 31), these letters present the doctrine of Christ in a distinct manner. They contain great passages which highlight the person and work of Christ in a definitive fashion (Col. 1:14-22, 2:3, 9-15; Phile. 15-20; Eph. 1:7-12; Phil. 2:5-11).

4. The Ecclesiological Letters: I Timothy, Titus, and II Timothy.

Date: about A.D. 63-67. The doctrine of the (local) church is the main theme of these last three letters of Paul, often called the Pastoral Epistles. They deal primarily with the responsibilities of the leaders of the churches. In them are found detailed instructions regarding the officers, administration, and activities of the church. The last days of Paul are reflected in the closing chapter of II Timothy.

I Thessalonians

Suggested Reading   I Thessalonians

On his second missionary journey, Paul arrived in Thessalonica, the capital of Macedonia (Acts 17:1-9). Things went well for the missionaries (Silas and Timothy were Paul's companions at this point) until jealous Jews raised a cry against them, charging them with acts "contrary to the decrees of Caesar, saying that there is another king, *one* Jesus" (17:7). Thus they were driven from the city. When Paul arrived later in Corinth (Acts 18), he wrote the letters to the troubled Thessalonican Christians, who had themselves become the objects of persecution since Paul's departure (I Thess. 2:14). In lieu of a personal visit (I Thess. 2:17, 18), the apostle expresses his thanks to God for the news of the firm stand of the believers, such news having been brought by Timothy (I Thess. 3:6-10).

OUTLINE

> I. Salutation, 1:1
> II. Thanksgiving, 1:2-10
> III. The Pauline Ministry Defended, 2:1—3:13
> IV. The Christian Walk Delineated, 4:1—5:24
> V. Conclusion, 5:25-28

PURPOSE AND CONTENT The Thessalonian Epistles are the only letters of Paul that do not contain an official title of the writer, simply his name (and Silvanus and Timothy) at the beginning. He writes, it would seem, as a personal friend and spiritual adviser to his spiritual children who find themselves beset by afflictions and tribulations. They are perplexed as to why such things should happen to them. Does God care? To encourage them Paul reminds them how he himself was shamefully treated when he came into their city (2:1, 2), and that he had "told you beforehand that we are to suffer affliction" (3:4). All such things are part of the purpose of God.

Since the apostle had departed, some of their number had died. What was to be their attitude toward death? Pagan religion from which they had turned (1:9) held little hope for the afterlife; rather it was a place of darkness and fear. Would they ever see their loved ones again? On the authority of "the word of the Lord" (4:15), Paul assures them that the dead and living saints shall be one day reunited and together "caught up in the clouds, to meet the Lord in the air" (4:17). This was a word of comfort, indeed. But, on the other hand, the Second Advent called for vigilance as well (5:6). Here is the application of the doctrine to the everyday life of the Christian.

In this letter Paul closes every chapter with some teaching regarding the return of the Lord. In 1:10, the believer is "to wait for his Son from heaven." Paul reminds his readers that they will be his "glory and joy" at the coming of the Lord (2:19, 20). In 3:13, it is the desire of the apostle that the Christians be established "unblamable in holiness before our God and Father, at the coming of our Lord Jesus with all his saints." A major section follows in 4:13-18, where Paul informs his readers of the reunion of the dead and living saints at the descent of the Lord from heaven, and the entrance into eternal bliss with Him. Finally, 5:23 pictures the believer "preserved entire, without blame at the coming of our Lord Jesus Christ." [5]

II Thessalonians

SUGGESTED READING   II Thessalonians

OUTLINE
    I. Salutation, 1:1, 2
   II. Anticipation of the Day of the Lord, 1:3-12
  III. Description of the Day of the Lord, 2:1-17
   IV. Exhortation to Prayer and Proper Conduct in View of the
       Day of the Lord, 3:1-16
    V. Conclusion, 3:17, 18

PURPOSE AND CONTENT   Between the time of the writing of the two letters a new problem had arisen. Apparently someone had caused concern on the part of the believers with regard to their relation to "the day of the Lord." Paul wrote that they "be not quickly shaken from your mind, nor yet be troubled, either by spirit, or by word, or by epistle as from us, as that the day of the Lord is just at hand" (2:2).

---

[5] The word translated "coming" in these passages literally meant "presence" in first-century usage. (Cf. II Cor. 10:10.) But it also came to mean "arrival" and was used of the coming of a dignitary to some part of his domain.

Why was it that the idea of "the day of the Lord" should disrupt their peace of mind? Probably because the aspect of this event most prominent in their thinking was that of tribulation, judgment, and destruction. Such a portrayal occurs in many of the related Old Testament passages from which the concept comes (Joel 1:15—2:11; Obad. 15, 16; Zeph. 1:14-18; Zech. 14:1-8). It was to be a time that would strike terror into the hearts of men. The Thessalonians had begun to wonder whether they also might fall victim to the day of judgment.

It would not be proper to say that there is a simple solution to a complex problem. The chronological relationships of eschatological events is not always made clear. To be more precise, would these believers find themselves caught in the precarious days of "the great tribulation" which was to come upon the earth? Or, would the Lord take them away before the judgment dawned?

First, there are certain things, said Paul, which must occur before the full force of God's eschatological judgment will be manifested. There will be apostasy from true religion (2:3); there will be the appearance of "the man of sin" (2:3); and, finally, there will be the removal of a present restrainer (2:6, 7). These will be definite indications of the approaching day of reckoning.

Second, the believers are to be awake and aware of conditions about them and strengthen themselves in their faith (I Thess. 5:4-8; II Thess. 2:15). Thus they will be fortified for any crisis.

Third, and most vital of all, Paul assures the Christians that God is in control, He is working out His purpose and they are kept within His hand (I Thess. 5:9, 10, 23, 24; II Thess. 1:11, 12; 2:13, 14). This is the ultimate assurance which the believer has. The Second Advent not only brings judgment, but blessing also. The prophets had spoken of this aspect, too, with regard to Israel (Joel 2:28-32; Mic. 4:1-5; Zeph. 3:9-20; Mal. 4:2, 3). Paul now informs his readers that they shall be with the Lord and shall share His victory over His enemies (1:7-10).

Again, as in the first letter, the apostle closes with a number of practical exhortations, especially dealing with the need for honest toil among the Christians. Some of them, thinking that the Lord was to come at once, had ceased working and were becoming a drag upon the rest of the community. An almost certain solution to that problem is given by Paul in 3:10, as he says, "If any will not work, neither let them eat." This is at once a good combination of Christian teaching and common sense. All are to work together while they wait together for the great day of His appearing.

---

⁶ Two further words are also used to describe the Lord's return in this epistle. In 1:7, "revelation" has reference to "the unveiling", the "showing forth" of the Lord. Cf. Rev. 1:7, for the effect. Also, in 2:8, "manifestation" relates to the "splendor," the "brightness" of His appearance. It will dazzle and destroy the great enemy, "the lawless one" who is the agent of Satan. Cf. Rev. 19:11-21.

Suggested Questions and Discussions

1. What three national cultures affected Paul's life?
2. Show the influence of these varied backgrounds upon Paul's life and ministry.
3. How did Paul's conversion affect his life and teaching?
4. Name four basic categories into which Paul's letters fall and name the letters in each.
5. State the doctrine primarily emphasized in each category.
6. What was Paul's experience in Thessalonica on his second missionary journey (Acts 17:1-9)?
7. Name two major problems dealt with by Paul in I Thessalonians.
8. With what subject does each chapter of the first Epistle close?
9. What doctrinal problem, which arose among believers between the writing of the two Thessalonian Epistles, influenced the content of the second Epistle?

Additional Exploration

1. To assist you in mastering the basic content of the Thessalonian letters, prepare your own outline of these two books.
2. List the passages in Thessalonians relating to Christ's Second Coming in the chronological order of events.
3. With the aid of a topical index, examine other Scripture portions to determine the manner of Christ's Second Coming.
4. List several qualities which are admirable about Paul's life, indicating which impress you most.
5. What features of Paul's conversion are characteristic of all conversions? In what ways was his conversion unique?
6. To assist you in deepening your dedication to the Lordship of Christ, list specific ways and means to live in light of His coming. Use the Thessalonian Epistles as a basis for your list.

Suggested Resources

BRUCE, F. F. *Paul and Jesus.* Grand Rapids: Baker Book House, 1974.
—————————. *Paul: Apostle of the Heart Set Free.* Grand Rapids: Eerdmans Publishing Co., 1978.
HIEBERT, D. EDMOND. *Thessalonian Epistles.* Chicago: Moody Press, 1971.
MORRIS, LEON. *The First and Second Epistles to the Thessalonians: New International Commentary on the New Testament.* Grand Rapids: Eerdmans Publishing Co., 1959.
WARD, R. A. *Commentary On First and Second Thessalonians.* Waco, TX: Word, 1974.

CHAPTER SIX

Pauline Epistles

I and II Corinthians

According to the previous classification of Paul's epistles, these letters are to be considered primarily soteriological, since they deal largely with the subject, salvation. Together with Galatians and Romans they form the heart of the Pauline writings. Even the radical critics, who have often rejected many of Paul's writings as authentic works, usually have accepted these letters as genuine. The core of Paul's preaching—faith in Christ and dedication to Him—is written large in all of them. His favorite expression, "in Christ," describing the new relationship of the regenerated individual to his Saviour and Lord, occurs again and again.

This correspondence emerges from the third missionary journey of Paul (cf. Acts 18:23—21:14). First Corinthians was written from Ephesus (I Cor. 16:7-9), while II Corinthians likely came from Macedonia (see II Cor. 2:12, 13; 7:5-7).

I Corinthians

SUGGESTED READING   I Corinthians 1—4, 8—10, 13, 15

BACKGROUND   Paul first visited Corinth on his second journey (Acts 18:1-17). While waiting for Silas and Timothy to come from Macedonia and rejoin him in Corinth, Paul met Aquila and Priscilla and, finding them to be tentmakers as he was, lived with them while carrying on his preaching.

Upon the arrival of his companions, carrying with them news of conditions to the North (in Thessalonica and Berea), Paul reemphasized his proclamation "that Jesus was the Christ" (i.e., Messiah). This brought about the usual reaction from the Jews and Paul henceforth concentrated on the Gentile ministry in Corinth (Acts 18:6). Before long a number of people became Christians, even including Crispus the ruler of the synagogue. For a period of at least eighteen months Paul continued a systematic teaching program among them.

The event that apparently led to the departure of the apostle from the city was his appearance before Gallio, the proconsul of Achaia, whose residence was in Corinth. As Gallio listened to the arguments of Paul's Jewish accusers, he manifested a stolid indifference. This was because it concerned matters of Jewish law, not Roman law, and his courtroom was not the place for religious disputes. It should be said that Gallio's indifference was in reality a blessing, for it diverted the actions of the Jews and set Paul free to continue his work.

While in Ephesus on his third journey (Acts 19:1-41), tidings were brought to Paul by some of the household of Chloe that things were not well in Corinth (I Cor. 1:11). In addition, a letter had been sent by the Corinthian church containing a number of problems to which they wished answers from the apostle (I Cor. 7:1; 8:1; 12:1; 15:12; 16:1). To reply to these and related matters, this first epistle was written.

OUTLINE

     I. Introduction, 1:1-9
     II. Reply to Reports from Chloe, 1:10—6:20
     III. Reply to the Letter from Corinth, 7:1—16:9
     IV. Conclusion, 16:10-24

PURPOSE AND CONTENT   The central concept of the letter is that redemption must be applied to everyday situations. The believer is to remember that the new life in Christ calls for a new way of living, the appeal being made to the relationship of the Holy Spirit to the believer (3:16, 17; 6:11, 19, 20).

It will help to emphasize these commands if one recalls the character of the city of Corinth. In the first century it was noted for its wickedness and immorality, highlighted by the corrupt, sensual worship of Aphrodite, the Greek goddess of love. Her temple, including a thousand religious prostitutes, stood in manifest contrast to the believer as "the temple of the Holy Spirit" and His demand for righteousness.

In the first section of the letter (chaps. 1—6), most of Paul's teaching deals with the problem of authority in the church. The Corinthian believers had been divided by various "religious loyalties." Some had appealed to Paul, the leading exponent of the doctrine of justification by faith and of the liberty of the Christian from the bondage of law. Too, he was the founder of this church. Others sided with Apollos, the learned teacher from Alexandria, filled with the knowledge of the Scriptures. He had followed Paul in his visit to Corinth (Acts 18:24—19:1). There were still others who held that Peter, one of the original disciples of the Lord, with his great love for Christ and his studied concern for the principles of the law of the Lord, was a worthy leader. And finally, there were those who piously looked askance at such discord, and exclaimed, "We simply follow Christ!" These last were indeed the worst of all, for they set themselves up above their brethren and sought to keep Christ all to themselves. Paul's crisp answer to all such disputes is given in 3:1-9. Along with this he calls upon them to gain true spiritual insight and to remember that they are responsible to God —both in the present and one day at the judgment seat (2:1-16; 3:10-23).

Two other matters, sexual immorality (5:1-13; 6:12-20) and lawsuits, (6:1-11) are dealt with in this section. Paul rebuked the church for not handling these matters themselves. The former is dealt with by a severe judgment which, however, is to result in the eventual reclaiming of the offender (5:3-5). The latter problem should be cared for, taught Paul, by the church, not in heathen courts. Lawsuits, in fact, are in themselves "a defect in you" (6:7). The final appeal is to maintain the unity and purity of the body of Christ.

In the second section of the letter (chaps. 7—16), a number of varied problems appear. The majority of the content, however, relates to the matter of spiritual relationships, either of believers to one another (chaps. 7—10) or to situations within the ministries of the church (chaps. 11—14). When dealing with the problems of marital relationships, Paul commands that its sanctity is to be maintained by those contemplating marriage, in the case of a divided household, and unmarried women. A spiritual basis is in evidence throughout the discussion.

When the problems of conscience are being faced, Paul sets forth a number of guiding principles.[1] First, nothing is to be permitted to remain in one's life if it causes another Christian to stumble (8:9, 13). Second, the preaching of the Gospel is not to be hindered, rather aided (9:12, 22). Third, all things are to be done "to the glory of God" (10:31).

The ministry of women in the church and the proper conditions for observing the Lord's supper are discussed in chapter 11. The nature and use of spiritual gifts is the burden of Paul in chapters 12—14. They are to be exercised in love (chap. 13) and all things are to "be done decently and in order" (14:40). This is necessary because all believers are members of the one Body (12:12-30). Therefore, if the unity of the Body is to be maintained, and if the work is to go forward, proper use of spiritual gifts is required.

Only in chapter 15 is a purely doctrinal issue discussed. This is the classic passage in the New Testament on the subject of the resurrection of the body. First, Christ's resurrection is described (vv. 1-19). Then, the application of this great truth is made (vv. 20-58). Because He came out of the grave, so shall all men in God's own time (v. 22). Paul describes the resurrection of the body. It shall be "a spiritual body" (v. 44), that is, characterized by spiritual rather than natural life. Even as our Lord's resurrection body, however, it will be a recognizable form. The great hope of the believer's resurrection is described in verses 50-58 (cf. I Thess. 4:13-18).

In closing this lengthy epistle, Paul reminds them, as he has done in the Galatian churches, of the collection he is receiving for the needy saints in

---

[1]These are matters which relate to personal habits and scruples and for which Scripture allows liberty, i.e., habits of eating, dress, the use of time and such. See also Rom. 14:1—15:13.

Jerusalem. That which they give is to be given regularly, voluntarily, and proportionately (16:1, 2).

II Corinthians

SUGGESTED READING   II Corinthians 1—3, 5, 10—13

PURPOSE   One of the most personal of Paul's letters, II Corinthians is, for the most part, a defense of Paul's ministry (chaps. 1—7) and his apostleship (chaps. 10—13). Chapters 8 and 9 consist of an added plea to fulfill their ministry of giving and a pointed reminder that they have been somewhat negligent in the fulfillment of their stewardship.

OUTLINE
     I. Salutation, 1:1, 2
     II. Problems of the Christian Ministry, 1:3—7:16
     III. Problems of Christian Giving, 8:1—9:15
     IV. Problems of a Christian Minister, 10:1—13:10
     V. Conclusion, 13:11-14

BACKGROUND   After having sent the First Epistle to the Corinthian Church, Paul waited at Ephesus for their response. He had then gone north to Troas to meet Titus, but when he did not appear he continued into Macedonia (2:12, 13). When they did meet, Paul wrote that he was comforted by the report of "your longing, your mourning, your zeal for me" (7:7). The news, however, was not all favorable. A vocal element in the church was inveighing against the authority of the apostle. Apparently a group of Jewish opponents (11:2), they discounted the reality of Paul's faith in Christ and the genuineness of his ministry (10:2) and despised his person (10:10). While there had been repentance on the part of some in the church (2:1-11), the unrepentant group continued to press hard upon Paul. Thus he bares his inmost feelings here in a way not seen in any other existing letter which he wrote.

CHARACTERISTIC   Amid the multitude of personal references, Paul has
FEATURES   given to the Church in this letter many important enduring doctrinal affirmations. Notice especially the leading references to the character and workings of God (1:3, 4; 2:14; 4:5, 6; 5:18-21; 6:14-18; 9:7-15), the contrast between the old and new covenants (chap. 3), the future state (5:1-10), the ministry of reconciliation (5:14-21), and Christian stewardship of money (chaps. 8, 9).

Suggested Questions and Discussions

1. Illustrate from these Corinthian Epistles the reasons it may be said that they form the heart of the Pauline writings.

2. Briefly summarize Paul's experiences in Corinth prior to writing I Corinthians.
3. What was the immediate occasion for Paul's writing I Corinthians?
4. What is the central concept of I Corinthians and how can it be fulfilled?
5. Illustrate from Paul's dealing with any three problems in the Corinthian church how Paul's solutions are applicable today.
6. Summarize the teaching of I Corinthians 15 concerning the Resurrection.
7. What was Paul's major purpose in writing II Corinthians?
8. Briefly summarize the background of II Corinthians.
9. List several important doctrinal emphases in II Corinthians.

Additional Exploration

1. Select a number of passages that might serve as maxims for a day (e.g., We are ambassadors for Christ). Some find spiritual help from listing a Scriptural maxim at the top of each day's list of "things to do."
2. Prepare a list with Scripture references of key doctrinal truths found in the Corinthian Epistles.
3. Discuss to what extent the ways Paul defended himself in II Corinthians 10—13 are applicable today.
4. List your significant roles in family and church life (i.e., husband, father, son, church member, and other). Under these headings list Scriptures from the Corinthian Epistles which state guiding principles for these specific roles.
5. For a fuller grasp of the Corinthian Epistles, read the remaining chapters not listed in *Suggested Reading*.

Suggested Resources

BRUCE, F. F. *First and Second Corinthians: The New Century Bible Commentary*. Grand Rapids: Eerdmans Publishing Co., 1980.

GODET, FREDERIC L. *Commentary on First Corinthians*. Grand Rapids: Kregel Pub., 1977.

HUGHES, PHILIP. *Commentary on the Second Epistle to the Corinthians*. Grand Rapids: Eerdmans Publishing Co., 1962.

MORRIS, L. *The First Epistle of Paul to the Corinthians: Tyndale New Testament Commentaries*. Grand Rapids: Eerdmans Publishing Co., 1958.

TASKER, R. V. G. *The Second Epistle of Paul to the Corinthians: Tyndale New Testament Commentaries*. Grand Rapids: Eerdmans Publishing Co., 1958.

CHAPTER SEVEN

Pauline Epistles

Galatians and Romans

Galatians

SUGGESTED READING   Galatians

Galatians and Romans give the emphasis to salvation that is found in the Corinthian Epistles. Galatians is a sturdy defense of the doctrine that "a man is not justified by the works of the law but through faith in Jesus Christ" (2:16). In no other writing has Paul set himself so forcibly to establish the genuineness of his apostolic commission and his message.

BACKGROUND   The questions of the date and destination, as well as the place of writing, of this letter are difficult to answer with any certainty. It may well have been the earliest of Paul's writings, penned soon after his first missionary journey upon his return to Syrian Antioch. Thus, it would be dated about 48/49. But the epistle has also been placed later by some (as late as 58, Lightfoot). Even the late date, of course, would still presuppose the lapse of a relatively short period of time after the founding of the Galatian churches.

While the letter is addressed to the churches of Galatia, the matter of destination is problematic due to the first-century meaning of the name itself. That is, "Galatia" could be understood in more than one way. This territory, located in eastern Asia Minor, was settled by the Gauls in the third century B.C. and took its name from these invaders. Eventually, after the Romans came into control of the area, the territory was enlarged, an area to the south was included with the northern section and the whole new province was called Galatia. When Paul wrote the letter, then, was he addressing people in North Galatia or in South Galatia? Most of the older commentators favor the former view; the majority of recent writers favor the latter view. Whichever is accepted, the message of Galatians remains unaffected.

OUTLINE   In examining the structure of the book, one may discern logical steps in Paul's argument. Once he has set the stage for what he has to say (1:1-10), he immediately plunges in to defend his position—that justification before God comes by faith and not by works and that Christ has set us free from the bondage of the law.

I. Introduction, 1:1-10

II. The Autobiographical Argument:
   the Gospel Revealed, 1:11—2:21
   A. Direct revelation of the Gospel, 1:11-24
   B. Apostolic confirmation of the Gospel, 2:1-10
   C. Personal application of the Gospel, 2:11-21

III. The Doctrinal Argument: the Gospel Prophesied, 3:1—4:31
   A. The personal appeal, 3:1-5
   B. The experience of Abraham, 3:6-14
   C. The promise and the law, 3:15-22
   D. The nature of sonship, 3:23—4:7
   E. The danger of defection, 4:8-20
   F. The lesson by allegory, 4:21-31

IV. The Practical Argument: the Gospel Applied, 5:1—6:10

V. Conclusion, 6:11-18

PURPOSE AND CONTENT   One cannot help but observe that there is no familiar and friendly introduction to this letter as is common in Paul's epistles. He states his business and gets into the details of the argument at once. Paul is amazed that these Christian congregations are so soon wavering in their loyalty to Christ and himself. He roundly condemns the "perverters of the gospel" (1:6, 7) and calls down the curse of God upon them (1:8, 9).

First, he himself has received his Gospel from Christ (1:11, 12). It has not been communicated to him by others; they have only concurred with him in his message and ministry (1:16—2:10). Therefore, on the basis of his own well established experience, he claims that his message is genuine.

Second, the Gospel is not a new thing; it was taught by the Old Testament (3:8). Abraham is the great example of justification by faith in God. As he came into this relationship long before the Law was given, the Law did not justify him—neither can it justify anyone (3:9-14). Paul elaborates this principle by contrasting the "child" with the "son" (3:23—4:7) and drawing upon the story of Abraham's two sons to teach the same truth allegorically (4:21-31).

Third, the Gospel works in personal experience (5:1). When applied, it gives the individual freedom from bondage to sin, victory over the flesh (the old nature within) and the ability to show forth works of righteousness. All this is set within the framework of the work of the Holy Spirit in the believer's life. "If we live by the Spirit, by the Spirit let us also walk" (5:25).

Thus, in Galatians, probably the earliest of Paul's writings, appears a powerful presentation of the nature of justification. The response of faith on the part of the sinner not only brings him right standing with God, but brings into his life the dynamic of the Spirit to work the works of God.

'The Gospel came to him from Christ (1:12); he also has a new relationship to Christ (2:20).

Romans
SUGGESTED READING   Romans

At the center of "the good tidings of great joy" which were spoken to the shepherds of Bethlehem was a Saviour, One who should redeem His people. This subject of redemption is defined and developed by Paul in his letter to the Romans, the most orderly and detailed treatment of salvation in the New Testament.

BACKGROUND   For many years the apostle had wanted to visit the Christians in Rome (15:23), desiring to establish them in the faith (1:11). While he had been heretofore hindered, he stood ready "to preach the gospel to you also that are in Rome" (1:13-15). On his third missionary journey, shortly before leaving Corinth (Acts 20:1-3), he wrote this letter in lieu of a visit, and sent it, apparently, by the hand of Phoebe of Cenchrae (16:1, 2). Soon afterward he was arrested in Jerusalem (Acts 21:27 ff.). Thus, as it turned out, he did arrive in Rome, but not as a free man (Acts 28:16).

OUTLINE   The theme of the letter is redemption (3:24). Five aspects of the subject are carefully developed by Paul.

I. Introduction, 1:1-17

II. Sin: the Need for Redemption, 1:18—3:20
A. Gentile sin, 1:18—2:16
B. Jewish sin, 2:17—3:8
C. Universal sin, 3:9-20

III. Justification: the Provision of Redemption, 3:21—5:21

IV. Sanctification: the Effect of Redemption, 6:1—8:39
A. The union with Christ, 6:1-23
B. The conflict of natures, 7:1-25
C. The victory by the Spirit, 8:1-39

V. Jew and Gentile: the Scope of Redemption, 9:1—11:36
A. Israel's past—God's judgment for sin, 9:1-33
B. Israel's present—God's offer of salvation, 10:1-21
C. Israel's future—God's promise of restoration, 11:1-36

VI. Service: the Fruit of Redemption, 12:1—15:13

VII. Conclusion and Greetings, 15:14—16:27

PURPOSE AND   Paul's introductory words combine many remarks of a
CONTENT   personal and a theological nature (1:1-17). He tells a good deal about himself. He is a bondservant of Christ, yet an apostle (1:1). His commission is to the nations (1:5). He is a man of prayer (1:9, 10), an earnest worker (1:13-15), and unashamed of the message which he proclaims (1:16). Along with this, he describes the

Gospel as being prophesied in the Old Testament (1:2), centered in the Son of God (1:3), God's "dynamite" which brings salvation to those who believe it (1:16), and containing a revelation of God's righteousness to the faithful ones (1:17).

The first major division of the epistle (1:18—3:20) delineates the sinful condition of man and demonstrates the universal need for redemption. Common to the descriptions of various classes of persons is a picture of spiritual and moral degeneration. Indeed, the former leads to the latter.

Man has turned away from God and fallen into idolatry (1:21-23), thus "God gave them up" (1:24, 26, 28). Some have condemned their fellowmen, but they are in reality worthy of condemnation themselves (2:1-3), for they practice the same things. God "will render to every man according to his works" (2:6). Gentiles, without the written law of the Jews, have the voice of conscience within (2:14, 15). With all his privileges, the Jew himself has not maintained his spiritual life and the name of God is blasphemed among the Gentiles because of Jewish failure (2:24, 25). The final verdict declares the guilt of all before the righteousness of God. By works "shall no flesh be justified in his sight" (3:20).

Then the provision of God is declared (3:21—5:21). Justification is the answer—and it is "through faith in Jesus Christ unto all them that believe" (3:22). God is able to maintain His own righteousness and yet declare the sinner righteous because of the redeeming work of Christ (3:24-26). To illustrate the principle of justification by faith, Paul draws upon the example of Abraham (as he had done earlier in Galatians), showing that Abraham's acceptance preceded both the institution of circumcision and the giving of the Law, thus it was by his faith alone that he was declared righteous (4:10-13). Having been justified, the sinner is able to realize some of its benefits (5:1-11) which accrue from the work of the Lord Jesus (5:12-21).

Next, the logical effect of redemption is discussed (6:1—8:39). The implications of the new relationship with God are far-reaching. A new life (6:11) and a new loyalty (6:12-14) should be manifested. Despite the constant demands of the old nature to dominate (7:24), there is victory through the work of the Holy Spirit (chap. 8). He empowers (8:16) and intercedes (8:26). Surely the Lord's promise is true, "My grace is sufficient for thee" (cf. II Cor. 12:9).

Following this, Paul makes clear the universal nature of the message (9:1—11:36). It is to both Jew and Gentile. Though God may have set aside His people Israel, He has not cast them off (11:1). He is sovereign and is only working out His purpose of redemption (9:19-32). There is yet a day of restoration and blessing for Israel (11:25-32). In the present day, the Gospel goes out to all and "whosoever shall call upon the name of the Lord shall be saved" (10:13).

In the last major division of the letter, the outworking of redemption is described (12:1—15:13). Beginning with a plea for complete dedication to the Lord (12:1, 2),[2] Paul goes on to show the varied responsibilities and relationships which the Christian has. He is to evaluate himself sanely in the light of the grace of God; to fulfill his ministry within the church (12:3-8); and to have proper relationships to other individuals (12:9-21), to government (13:1-7), to society (13:8-14), and to Christians who differ with him in personal scruples (14:1—15:13).

The concluding words are largely personal in nature, consisting of the hopes and plans of the apostle, especially with reference to his visit to Rome, and a list of greetings to friends and fellow-workers in the church (15:14—16:27).

Suggested Questions and Discussions

1. What significant doctrine does Galatians clearly defend?
2. State the basic claims presented by Paul in Galatians as to the genuineness of his message.
3. What was the occasion of Paul's writing the Epistle to the Romans?
4. What Old Testament character does Paul use in Romans and Galatians to illustrate justification by faith? What is the significance of the time he appeared in Old Testament sequence?
5. According to Galatians 5:1-24 and Romans 6—8, how does a Christian live a spiritual life?
6. How can a man be justified by God? (Rom. 3:21—5:21.)
7. Referring to the outline and Scripture divisions of the book of Romans, summarize briefly Israel's past, present, and future.
8. State some of the main responsibilities which the Christian has in doing the will of God (Romans 12—15).

Additional Exploration

1. For a better comprehension of Romans and Galatians, expand the outlines.
2. Utilizing your Bible concordance or index, contrast the use of the words *law* and *grace* or *faith* and *works* in the Bible.
3. In a panel discussion, consider ways in which Christian liberties are sometimes abused and suggest remedies.
4. Using verses only from the book of Romans, outline the steps leading to salvation.
5. Referring to interpretive news periodicals such as *Newsweek* and *Time*, trace significant developments in contemporary history which appear to be fulfillment of prophecy concerning the Jews. Why should the Christian be alert to these?

Suggested Resources

BRUCE, F. F. *The Epistle of Paul to the Romans: Tyndale New Testament Commentaries.* Grand Rapids: Eerdmans Publishing Co., 1963.

MOULE, H. C. G. *Studies in Romans.* Grand Rapids: Kregel Pub., 1977.

TENNEY, MERRILL C. *Galatians: The Charter of Christian Liberty.* Rev. ed. Grand Rapids: Eerdmans Publishing Co., 1960.

---

[2]The word "present" denotes an act of sacrifice; the words "be transformed" represent a process, a continual change from within. The latter is the basis for our English word "metamorphosis."

CHAPTER EIGHT

Pauline Epistles

Colossians, Philemon, Ephesians, and Philippians

A misfortune or a blessing? How is Paul's imprisonment to be viewed? Would it have been better for all concerned if Paul had remained a free man and able to carry on his missionary travels? Or, did God direct Paul into such a situation as this? Possibly the question may never be settled to the satisfaction of all, but this point is clear: the period which Paul spent in the Roman prison (Acts 28:30, 31) was one of the richest of his career. It provided him an entrance into the household of the emperor (Phil. 1:13; 4:22) and brought forth the so-called "Prison Epistles" the most profound and Christ-exalting of Paul's written works.

Each of these letters contains references to his situation. In Colossians 1:24 and 4:18, he speaks of his "sufferings" and his "bonds." Philemon 1, 9, 10 refer to him as a prisoner and one in bonds. Again, in Ephesians 3:1; 4:1; 6:20, he makes mention of being a prisoner and "in a chain." Finally, Philippians 1:12, 13 calls attention to his bonds and the presence of the whole praetorian guard. The place of his imprisonment has been traditionally held to have been Rome.

Colossians

SUGGESTED READING   Colossians

Here is one of two epistles written by Paul to churches which he did not personally found. It seems likely that during his lengthy stay at Ephesus (Acts 19) the message of Christ had been taken to Colossae by one of his fellow-workers. He describes Epaphras, a Colossian Christian serving with Paul (4:12), as "our beloved fellow-servant, who is a faithful minister of Christ on our behalf, who also declared unto us your love in the Spirit" (1:7, 8).

BACKGROUND   Colossae did not rank with Ephesus in either size or importance. It was an inland city, lying beside the Lycus River, near Laodicea and Hierapolis (cf. 4:13). Located on the main commercial thoroughfare between East and West, the city was influenced by contrasting ideologies. These influences seem to be reflected in the epistle as Paul writes descriptively of the person of Christ (cf. 1:14-20) and to correct the current errors relating to redemption and the pattern of Christian living (2:8—3:4).

The name usually given to the false teaching in this city is "the Colossian heresy." It apparently consisted of a mixture of Jewish and Gnostic ideas, combined to create a threat to the Gospel of Christ. This unsound teaching sought to reduce Christianity to a legal system and to obscure the person and work of Christ. Paul attacks the errors at Colossae by the clear presentation of counter truths. The key verse is 1:18—"that in all things he might have the pre-eminence."

OUTLINE

    I. Salutation, 1:1, 2
   II. The Prayer of Thanksgiving, 1:3-8
  III. The Prayer of Intercession, 1:9-14
   IV. The Supremacy of Christ, 1:15-23
    V. Paul's Desire for the Saints, 1:24—2:7
   VI. Paul's Exhortations to the Saints, 2:8—4:6
  VII. Paul's Representatives to Colossae, 4:7-9
 VIII. Greetings, 4:10-17
   IX. Conclusion, 4:18

COMPARISON WITH EPHESIANS   As one reads this epistle, he may be impressed with its likeness to Ephesians. Indeed, they may be called the twin epistles of the New Testament. They are most nearly alike in their presentation of Christ and His Body, the Church. In Colossians, He is "the head of the body" (1:18); in Ephesians, it is "the church, which is his body" (1:22, 23). The development in Colossians, then, concentrates on the exalted position of Christ; in Ephesians, upon the nature of the Church.

Another likeness which is notable is the section dealing with the application of the Gospel to practical affairs. Both epistles describe the old man and the new man together with the evidences of each (Col. 3:9, 10; Eph. 4:22-24). Also, each contains commands to the various members of the household to fulfill their rightful functions (Col. 3:18—4:1; Eph. 5:22—6:9).

PURPOSE AND CONTENT   The key passages telling of Christ are to be found in 1:15-23 and 2:8—3:4. In the first, Christ is described as pre-eminent in at least four distinct relationships: to God (1:15); to created things (1:16, 17); to the Church (1:18); and, to the work of redemption (1:19-23). This discussion is preliminary and necessary to the exposing of the heresy described in chapter 2. The presentation of the superiority of Christ is the answer to all such errors. This is Paul's basic approach in the section which follows.

In reading 2:8—3:5, the main characteristics of this false teaching seem to be: (1) *Rationalistic philosophy* which denied revelation (2:8). Christ as the fullness of God, and the One in whom the Christian is "made full" is the answer (2:9). (2) *Legalistic religion* which was seriously endangering the concept of Christian liberty (2:16). Christ is the reality, the fulfillment of the types and shadows of ceremonial religion, says Paul (2:17). In Him, they are done away. (3) *Voluntary humility* and worship of angels, based on a superior knowledge (2:18). Christ is the Head (2:19). If He is not given His proper place, things will come in which are in reality useless for spiritual life (2:23).

Finally, Paul shows the implications of these teachings. A new kind of life, a new way of living is demanded (3:5-17). The one in whom "the word of Christ dwells richly" will give evidence of this new life (3:16, 17). Special emphasis is given to domestic relationships:

WIVES—be in subjection to your husbands (3:18)

HUSBANDS—love your wives (3:19)

CHILDREN—obey your parents (3:20)

FATHERS—do not provoke your children (3:21)

SERVANTS—obey your masters; you really serve Christ (3:22-25)

MASTERS—treat your servants justly (4:1)

Thus, Christ is not only to be pre-eminent in one's doctrine, but in his duties as well.

Philemon

SUGGESTED READING   Philemon

BACKGROUND   Along with constituting a part of the New Testament canon, this brief epistle is a prime example of Paul's personal correspondence. It is a letter written by one Christian to another, asking that a favor be granted because of their mutual relationship to Christ and to each other. It is a masterful example of the tactful approach to a delicate and difficult situation. The letter was sent along with Colossians to Philemon, in whose house the Colossian Church met.

OUTLINE
> I. Salutation, 1-3
> II. The Prayer for Philemon's Ministry, 4-7
> III. The Petition for Onesimus' Restoration, 8-21
> IV. The Prospect of Paul's Visit, 22
> V. Conclusion, 23-25

PURPOSE   Within the framework of Christology, Paul here illustrates the principle of forgiveness and restoration on the basis of substitution. He asks that Onesimus, the slave who is worthy of punishment, be forgiven by his master and received back "no longer as a servant, but more than a servant, a brother beloved" (16). Paul beseeches, and himself offers to pay any debt which stands due to Philemon (18, 19). Thus the doctrine of *imputation* is illustrated. The merit of one person is reckoned to the account of another.[1]

Ephesians

SUGGESTED READING   Ephesians

BACKGROUND   Ephesus, in the first century A.D., called herself the first city of Asia. Although the ancient city of Pergamum (cf. Rev. 2:12), just to the north, was still the official capital of the province, Ephesus had risen rapidly in stature. An important center commercially, intellectually, and religiously, she boasted one of the seven wonders of the ancient world: the ornate, glistening temple of Diana, the great goddess of the Ephesians (cf. Acts 19:23 ff.).

The history of the Ephesian Church may be traced in some detail through the New Testament. (1) Paul founded and established the work (Acts 19, 20). Having received the apostle's teaching for over two years, she was well grounded in the faith. (2) The Ephesian epistle reflects the spiritual capacity of this church. Paul was able to "feed them with strong meat." (Notice especially Eph. 1:3-14.) Further, the letter warns against the conflict with evil spirits (6:10 ff.), so prevalent a menace in this city (cf. Acts 19:11-17). (3) The letters to Timothy, who was left here by Paul to carry on the work (I Tim. 1:3 ff.), show the next stage in the history. False teachers had begun to trouble the believers and Paul sends instructions regarding sound teaching and the proper organization of the church. (4) In Revelation 2:1-7, the last chapter is written concerning this church in the New Testament. It is a sad word—she has "left her first love" for Christ (2:4). When she did not repent of her condition, as church history shows, she was removed—her lampstand no longer shone as a witness in Ephesus.

OUTLINE   The central theme of the epistle is the Church as the Body of Christ. Paul has given a sublime presentation of this truth from the very inception of the Church to its witness within the world and its conflict against the forces of evil.

    I. Salutation, 1:1, 2
    II. The Church in the Purpose of God, 1:3-14
    III. The Church and the Power of God, 1:15—2:10
    IV. The Church as the Household of God, 2:11-22
    V. The Church as the Revelation of God, 3:1-13
    VI. The Church and the Fullness of God, 3:14-21

---

[1]The expression, "put that to mine account," was a standard one in bookkeeping in the first century. It referred to making an entry in the ledger. Sometimes the word is translated "reckon." Cf. Rom. 4:3-5.

PURPOSE AND   The letter is addressed to the saints and the faithful ones,
CONTENT   two descriptions of the believer. One emphasizes his position in Christ, the other his character before God.

In the first part of the epistle (1:3-14) Paul concisely describes the origin of the Church, here in its universal aspect, in the purpose of God. He highlights such important themes as election (1:4), foreordination (1:5, 11), adoption (1:5), redemption (1:7), purpose (1:9, 10), and the sealing with the Holy Spirit (1:13), culminating in the final possession of the Church by God (1:14).[2]

By God's power the Church has been called into being (1:15—2:10) and is described as a great household, consisting of both Jew and Gentile (2:11-22), sharing alike in the riches of God's inheritance (3:1-13). God dwells within the Church which has been built upon a solid foundation and is being made up of many parts, each having its own place in the structure (2:19-22).

Characteristic in the practical division of the book (4:1—6:24) are the two concepts of "walk" and "warfare." While the word "walk," denoting one's manner of life, appears twice in the early chapters (2:2, 10), it is more common in the last part (4:1, 17; 5:2, 8, 15). The Christian is to "walk worthy," "walk not as the unbelievers," "walk in love," "walk as children of light," and "walk wisely." He is to walk in keeping with his position as a member of the Body of Christ (cf. I John 2:5, 6).

The exhortations to the members of the household are generally lengthier than in the Colossian letter. In Ephesians, Paul gives most attention to the wife-husband relationship, using it as an illustration of Christ and of the Church (5:32).[3] An abbreviated comparison of the two passages should make apparent the leading features of each:

Refs.	Ephesians	Refs.	Colossians
5:22-24	*Wives*: be subject to your own husbands.	3:18	*Wives*: be subject to your husbands.
5:25-31	*Husbands*: love your wives; notice Christ's example.	3:19	*Husbands*: love your wives; do not be bitter against them.
6:1-3	*Children*: obey your parents; it is God's command.	3:30	*Children*: obey your parents. This is the right thing to do.
6:4	*Fathers*: provoke not your children, but nurture them.	3:21	*Fathers*: provoke not your children, lest they be discouraged.

---

[2]Notice in this paragraph the repetition of the phrase "unto the praise of his glory" (1:6, 12, 14), distinguishing the work of the Father (vv. 3-6), the Son (vv. 7-12), and the Holy Spirit (vv. 13, 14) in the creation of the Church.

[3]In Col. Paul gives most attention to the "servant-master" relationship. (Cf. Paul's letter to Phile.)

Refs.	Ephesians	Refs.	Colossians
6:5-8	Servants: be obedient to your masters; serve the Lord.	3:22-25	Servants: be obedient to your masters; work heartily, as unto the Lord.
6:9	Masters: serve the Lord; forbear threatening; you have a Master in heaven.	4:1	Masters: render just and equal dues to your servants; you have a Master in heaven.

In closing this epistle, the apostle deals with the Christian's warfare (literally, wrestling, hand-to-hand combat) against the spiritual forces of darkness (6:10-20). His provision against this foe is the whole armor of God. If he will use it, it will enable him "to stand against the wiles of the devil" (v. 11), Paul describes the various pieces of the armor and the function of each.

Thus, while the Christian finds himself "in the heavenlies" (1:3, 10, 20; 2:6; 3:10; 6:12), he is also to avail himself of all God's provisions and give careful heed to all His demands for his life and warfare upon the earth.

Philippians

SUGGESTED READING   Philippians

"Rejoice in the Lord always: again I will say, Rejoice" (4:4). This note characterizes the Philippian letter. A proper appreciation of Paul's great faith in God makes joy seem a natural expression in spite of adverse circumstances.

BACKGROUND   The city of Philippi was the starting point for the preaching of the Gospel in Europe. Paul had sailed from Troas, following the Macedonian vision (Acts 16:9), "concluding that God had called us to preach the gospel unto them" (Acts 16:10). He had arrived in a city which had an illustrious history. It was on this site that, in 42 B.C., the famous battle was fought between Octavian and Antony over against Brutus and Cassius. Following the battle, the status of a Roman colony was conferred upon the city by the victorious Octavian. Thus it came to be modeled after the imperial city of Rome. The people were proud of their rights of citizenship (Acts 16:20, 21). Through the city ran the famous Via Egnatia, the trade route between East and West.

When Paul, Silas, Timothy, and Luke arrived here, they preached first to a group of women gathered for prayer near the river (Acts 16:13). These, among them Lydia and her family, later constituted the nucleus of the church in the city. Soon, however, trouble arose. When Paul and Silas ex-

---

'The term "wiles" (v. 11) is literally "strategy" or "methods" or "plans of attack." The companion expression, "fiery darts" (v. 16) refers to attacks of Satan upon the Christian; the "putting into operation" of the strategy.

pelled a demon from a slave girl, her masters seeing their gain from her services was gone (Acts 16:19) had the two imprisoned on a false charge. But an earthquake during the night liberated them from prison, their jailer became a Christian (Acts 16:34), and their appeal to their Roman citizenship freed them from further punishment (cf. Acts 16:22-24, 38-40). Years later, at the time of the writing of this letter, Paul was a prisoner again! This time, due to false accusations also, he had been sent to Rome in chains. Yet, he penned an epistle which radiates joy and speaks often of the good tidings, the Gospel of Christ. This is a demonstration of his testimony, "For to me to live is Christ" (Phil. 1:21).

OUTLINE   As the epistle is composed of many personal matters, the structure is not as clear-cut as many of his other writings. The underlying theme, however, is "the gospel" and the key words are "joy" and "rejoice."

    I. Salutation, 1:1, 2
    II. Thanksgiving and Prayer for the Saints, 1:3-11
    III. Paul and His Circumstances, 1:12-26
    IV. Believers and Their Conduct, 1:27-30
    V. Christ and His Example: Humility, 2:1-18
    VI. Timothy and Epaphroditus and Their Concern, 2:19-30
    VII. Paul and His Example: Maturity, 3:1—4:1
    VIII. Exhortations and Appreciation, 4:2-20
    IX. Conclusion, 4:21-23

PURPOSE AND CONTENT   Viewing the major features of the letter, one is readily able to see that the chief hortatory sections deal with the concepts of *unity through humility* (2:1-18) and *maturity in Christ* (3:1—4:1), and a number of specific applications of the latter in 4:2-20. The main personal sections concern Paul himself (1:12-26; 3:4-14; 4:10-20) and two of his fellow-workers, Timothy and Epaphroditus (2:19-30). The leading doctrinal passage concerns the incarnation and exaltation of Christ (2:5-11). In every kind of situation, Christ is exalted: in Paul's own sufferings (1:12-26); in the Christian's personal life (2:1-5); in Paul's own desires and ambitions (3:7-14); and in his realization of true serenity (4:10-18).

By His own example, Christ has shown the way of acceptance with God. The lowly place precedes the exalted position. Though the qualities of deity were resident within Him (2:6), He willingly relinquished His prerogatives to accomplish the work of the Cross (2:7, 8). Thus, God exalted Him to the supreme place over every creature; to Him every knee must bow (2:9-11). This is the Christ whom Paul desires to know in daily experience (3:10), and the One whom we await from heaven "Who shall change our vile body . . . like unto his glorious body" (3:20, 21).

Suggested Questions and Discussions

1. Why are Colossians, Philemon, Ephesians, and Philippians called Prison Epistles?
2. What was the Colossian heresy?
3. List several reasons for calling Colossians and Ephesians the twin epistles of the New Testament.
4. In the book of Colossians, with what major domestic relationships does Paul deal?
5. How is the doctrine of imputation illustrated in the book of Philemon?
6. Briefly trace the history of the Ephesian church as portrayed in the New Testament.
7. What is the central theme of the book of Ephesians?
8. Name at least three of Paul's experiences in Philippi prior to his writing the Philippian epistle.
9. Why was it possible for Paul to have the major theme which he had in his letter to the Philippians in spite of his experiences?

Additional Exploration

1. In each of the epistles studied in this chapter, find one or more significant indications of Paul's attitude during the days of his imprisonment.
2. Utilizing especially key phrases from these four epistles, draw a word portrait of Christ. *OR* Expand the chart you prepared in chapter I, project 1.
3. Trace specific scriptural commands and guiding principles that apply directly to your various roles in life. *OR* Expand the chart begun in chapter VI, project 4.
4. For personal enrichment, trace and summarize the use of the words "in Christ" as found in Ephesians and Colossians.
5. Prepare your own outline for one or more of the epistles covered in this chapter.

Suggested Resources

KENT, HOMER A., JR. *Ephesians, The Glory of the Church.* Winona Lake, IN: BMH Books, 1971.

MARTIN, R. P. *The Epistle of Paul to the Philippians: Tyndale New Testament Commentaries.* Grand Rapids: Eerdmans Publishing Co., 1960.

McDONALD, H. D. *Commentary on Colossians and Philemon.* Waco, TX: Word, 1980.

MOULE, H. C. G. *Colossian and Philemon Studies.* Minneapolis: Klock & Klock, 1981.

——————— *Studies in Ephesians.* Grand Rapids: Kregel Pub., 1977.

——————— *Studies in Philippians.* Grand Rapids: Kregel Pub., 1977.

SIMPSON, E. K. and BRUCE, F. F. *Epistles to the Ephesians and Colossians: New International Commentary on the New Testament.* Grand Rapids: Eerdmans Publishing Co., 1958.

CHAPTER NINE

Pauline Epistles

I Timothy, Titus, and II Timothy

The last group of epistles in the Pauline collection have been named the Pastoral Epistles because of their emphases on the personal responsibilities and the public functions of the pastor (literally, shepherd) of the local church. Written to two of Paul's closest companions, Timothy and Titus, they are the latest of Paul's letters, usually dated near the end of his life, about A.D. 63-67. Especially in II Timothy he seems to anticipate the end (cf. 4:6).

AUTHORSHIP Although scholars are divided on the matter of the authorship of these books, the three letters are here assumed to be Pauline.[1] They reflect Paul's life between the time of his imprisonment mentioned in Acts and his death some years later.

I Timothy

SUGGESTED READING   I Timothy

BACKGROUND Apparently converted under the preaching of Paul on his first mission to Galatia, Timothy enters the pages of the New Testament in Acts 16:1 ff. As Paul made a return journey into the same territory he found Timothy, likely in Lystra. He is called by the apostle "my true child in faith" (I Tim. 1:2) and "my beloved child" (II Tim. 1:2). Having been reared by his mother, a Jewess (although his father was a Greek, Acts 16:1, 3), he knew the Old Testament Scriptures from his childhood (II Tim. 3:14, 15) and now, being converted to Christianity, was "well reported of by the brethren that were at Lystra and Iconium" (Acts 16:2).

He accompanied Paul from this time onward, being left later in Ephesus to straighten out the affairs of the church, particularly some doctrinal difficulties, and to oversee its organization and deportment (cf. I Tim. 1:3 ff.; 3:1-14; 4:6-16). When Paul wrote to him from Rome, he asked Timothy to come soon to visit him, bringing John Mark with him and also some personal

---

[1]For a readable discussion, see D. Guthrie, *The Pastoral Epistles*, pp. 11-52. A slightly more technical approach is taken in W. Hendricksen, *Exposition of the Pastoral Epistles*, pp. 4-33.

belongings (II Tim. 4:9, 11, 13). We do not know whether or not Timothy arrived before Paul's death.

From the contents of these letters, as well as scattered references in other epistles, Timothy may be pictured as a faithful, diligent worker, dear to Paul's heart (cf. Phil. 2:19, 20). The fact that the great apostle entrusted Timothy with the responsibility of a leading church, bears testimony to his confidence in his companion. It may also be concluded that Timothy needed occasional prodding and encouragement by Paul, possibly due to a natural timidity (cf. II Tim. 1:6, 7; I Tim. 4:12-16). As a "man of God" (I Tim. 6:11), he was exhorted to emulate his Lord "who before Pontius Pilate witnessed the good confession" (6:13) and to "guard that which is committed unto *thee"* (6:20).

PURPOSE The letter has a double aspect. One is the emphasis upon Timothy as a person—he has certain responsibilities to fulfill as a minister of the Lord and as an exemplary individual. The other is the emphasis upon his official responsibilities—he is to see that the church is properly taught, organized, and administered. The former aspect is seen particularly in 1:3-7, 18-20; 4:6-16; 5:1 ff.; 6:11-21; the latter particularly in chapters 2, 3, 5 and 6:1-10. As might be expected, there is not a hard and fast line between the two. Personal and official responsibilities cannot logically be separated.

OUTLINE

    I. Salutation, 1:1, 2
    II. Charge to Timothy, 1:3-20
    III. Exhortations for Church order:
        Prayer and Worship, 2:1-15
    IV. Requirements for Church Officers:
        Elders and Deacons, 3:1-13
    V. Parenthesis, 3:14-16
    VI. Instructions for Church Activities, 4:1—6:21a
    VII. Conclusion, 6:21b

BASIC FEATURES As more will be said about Timothy himself in the second letter, special attention is given here to the basic features of church organization and administration.

First, the ideal church should be characterized by *proper prayer life* (chap. 2). Regulations for the objects of prayer is first given (vv. 1-4), then for the respective functions of men and women in the church (vv. 8-15). Emphasis is upon the proper attitudes in prayer and service, rather than upon outward appearances. Men are assigned the place of official teachers and administrators.

Second, the ideal church should be characterized by *proper organization* (3:1-13). The requirements for elders, deacons, and the women (deaconesses?) are enumerated in this passage. They relate both to the moral and spiritual qualities of the person desiring an office, and to the functions which he is expected to perform. The first-century church held high standards, indeed.

Third, the ideal church should be characterized by *proper administration* of its various affairs (5:1—6:10). Emphasis is placed here first upon the care and responsibilities of the widows (5:3-16). If a widow is aged and desolate, let the church care for her. If she has children or grandchildren, let them care for her. If she is a young widow, Paul recommends remarriage and rearing of a family. Following this, instructions are given regarding the work of the elders (5:17-25), the servants (6:1, 2), and the teachers (6:3-10). Each is to discharge his responsibilities knowing that he is answerable to the Lord.

Titus

SUGGESTED READING   Titus

BACKGROUND   Like Timothy, Titus too appears to have been led to Christ by Paul. The apostle calls him "my true child after a common faith" (Titus 1:4). He was a Greek, possibly from Syrian Antioch. When Paul and Barnabas went from Antioch to Jerusalem to discuss their ministry with the leaders of the church there, Titus accompanied them (Gal. 2:1-3). There he is presented as an example of a Gentile become Christian without the necessity of Jewish circumcision. He thus illustrates the principle of which Paul speaks in Galatians 2:16.

Strange as it may seem, the name of Titus does not appear in the Book of Acts. Of all the major companions of the Apostle, only he and Luke are not mentioned there by name, although Luke is included anonymously in the "we sections."

The chief picture which we gain of Titus, aside from the references in the epistle which bears his name, is to be found in II Corinthians. He seems to have been the kind of person we today call a trouble shooter, thus he was sent by Paul into difficult situations to attempt a solution. Paul rejoices, as he writes to the Corinthians, in that he was comforted by the return of Titus from Corinth because the apostle's hopes for the church seem to have been justified. Apparently Titus had been successful in smoothing the troubled waters (II Cor. 7:6-10, 13-16). Then, too, he had been sent to see about the promised contribution for the Jerusalem church. Having been lax in fulfilling this ministry, the Corinthians were urged by Paul to demonstrate to his fellow-workers "the proof of your love, and of our glorying on your behalf" (cf. 8:6, 16, 17, 23, 24).

We see in the Epistle to Titus that Paul had left his companion in the island of Crete to "set in order the things that were wanting, and appoint elders in every city" (1:5). As in the case of Timothy in Ephesus, Titus was given the responsibility of organizing and administering the affairs of these churches, together with carrying on a sound program of teaching. His last appearance in the New Testament is in II Timothy 4:10 where he has left Rome and gone to Dalmatia, apparently to represent Paul once again.

The epistle itself has as its theme "sound (literally, "healthful") doctrine" (cf. 1:9; 2:1; also 2:7, 8). Proper understanding of the truth should eventuate in good works (cf. 1:16; 2:7, 14; 3:1, 8, 14). The good works are not the basis of salvation (3:5) but are to be the evidence of it (3:8).

OUTLINE

    I. Salutation, 1:1-4
    II. Paul's Instructions to Titus, 1:5—3:11
        A. Regarding the churches, 1:5-16
        B. Regarding individuals, 2:1-15
        C. Regarding the world, 3:1-8
        D. Regarding heresies, 3:9-11
    III. Personal Notes, 3:12-14
    IV. Conclusion, 3:15

PURPOSE AND CONTENT It appears that the chief problem in Crete came from false teachers, mainly, "of the circumcision" (i.e., Jewish), who are described by Paul as "unruly men, vain talkers and deceivers" (1:10). They were teaching "Jewish fables" (1:14) and introducing "foolish questionings, and genealogies, and strifes, and fightings about the law" (3:9). Along with this were the moral laxity of the Cretans (1:12, 13), and the careless demeanor of some of the members of the church (2:2, 3, 10; 3:2). To counteract such vanities, Paul urges upon Titus the need for sound doctrine, emphasizing that the Word of God is the basis for the Christian life (cf. 1:3; 2:5, 10). When this teaching is properly received, good works should result.

The doctrine of God is prominent in the epistle, also. Several of the references relate to the Father (1:1, 3, 4; 2:10; 3:4); others to the Son (1:4; 2:13; 3:6); and to the Holy Spirit (3:5).

The doctrine of salvation is central in 2:11-14 and 3:4-7. The grace of God not only saves, but also instructs the believer and gives him the blessed hope. Those who have been redeemed are to show a change in character (v. 14). Notice, too, the four important words describing God's character in relation to salvation: kindness, love (3:4), mercy (3:5), and grace (3:7).

As compared with I Timothy, the instructions regarding church officers are more brief in Titus. Here only the elder (or, bishop) is described; the deacons are not mentioned. Once again the need for men of high spiritual and moral qualities is stressed. They must be both exemplary in character and capable in their functions. "In all things shewing thyself a pattern of good works . . . that they may adorn the doctrine of God our Saviour in all things" (2:7a, 10b).

II Timothy

SUGGESTED READING   II Timothy

BACKGROUND   At the time of the writing of this letter, Paul was awaiting execution. According to tradition, he was imprisoned in the Mamertine dungeon in Rome, under circumstances much less favorable than those of Acts 28:30. He seems to expect death rather than release (4:6; contrast Phil. 1:19; Phile. 22).

PURPOSE AND   Thus these are the final recorded words of Paul in the
CONTENT   New Testament. With special interest we look into these pages for thoughts of the great apostle as he faces the end of his life and ministry. As he faces death alone, except for the companionship of Luke the physician (4:11), his chief concern is for the welfare of Timothy and the success of his work in Ephesus. The leading exhortations which appear throughout the letter are worthy of careful attention:

"Stir up the gift of God, which is in thee" (1:6)
"Be not ashamed . . . but suffer hardship" (1:8)
"Hold the pattern of sound words" (1:13)
"Guard that good thing committed unto thee" (1:14)
"Commit the things which you have heard to others" (2:2)
"Of these things put them in remembrance" (2:14)
"Give diligence to present thyself approved unto God" (2:15)
"Flee youthful lusts" (2:22)
"Abide . . . in the things which thou hast learned" (3:14)
"Preach the word" (4:2)
"Be . . . sober . . . fulfil thy ministry" (4:5)

These constitute the major thrust of the epistle. It is a letter of personal counsel.

OUTLINE

        I. Salutation, 1:1, 2
      II. Thanksgiving for Timothy, 1:3-18
    III. Exhortations to Timothy, 2:1-26
    IV. Warnings to Timothy, 3:1-17
     V. The Final Charge to Timothy, 4:1-8
    VI. Personal Instructions to Timothy, 4:9-21
   VII. Conclusion, 4:22

CHARACTERISTIC   Brief consideration should be given to two or three of
FEATURES   the outstanding passages in the epistle. Chapter 2 is characterized by the seven metaphors which are used to describe the believer. Paul, by the use of these varied figures of speech, makes clear to Timothy the differing facets of the Christian's ministry and

the responsibility connected with each.

As a *child,* he is to be strong and active (vv. 1, 2)

As a *soldier,* he is to suffer hardship and
also please his superior (vv. 3, 4)

As an *athlete,* he is to obey the rules of the game (v. 5)

As a *husbandman* (farmer), he is to labor and
thus have full participation in the results (v. 6)

As a *workman,* he is to be diligent,
rightly handling the Word of God (v. 15)

As a *vessel,* he is to be honorable, ready for the Master's use (v. 21)

As a *servant,* he is to be gentle and helpful (vv. 24, 25)

In 3:14-17, one of the classic passages on the nature of the Scriptures appears. The nature of the Scriptures, i.e., the written Word, is divine; they are "inspired of God." God has "breathed them out" to men; the result is His Word communicated faithfully. They are able (1) to enlighten one unto salvation (v. 15) and to thoroughly equip the man of God (v. 17).

The letter ends with a series of personal remarks, including the request that Timothy visit him soon (4:9), before the winter season if possible (4:21). While in his prison cell he wanted his cloak for warmth and his books for study. To the very end of his life Paul remained active and alert. "I have fought the good fight, I have finished the course, I have kept the faith: henceforth there is laid up for me the crown of righteousness, which the Lord, the righteous judge, shall give to me at that day" (4:7, 8).

Suggested Questions and Discussions

1. Why are these epistles called the Pastoral Epistles? Illustrate your answer with references from the letters.
2. What was Timothy's family and spiritual background prior to his joining Paul in ministry?
3. Describe the characteristics of Timothy as a Christian worker.
4. How did Paul show his confidence in Timothy?
5. What three basic features should characterize the Church according to I Timothy?
6. In what ways did Titus demonstrate his abilities as a problem solver?
7. What is the theme of the book of Titus?
8. In what ways were false teachers causing problems in Crete?
9. State several of the leading exhortations of Paul to Timothy as found in II Timothy.
10. List several of the metaphors Paul uses in II Timothy to describe the believer.

Additional Exploration

1. Compile some maxims for Christians as found in II Timothy. *OR* Expand your list of maxims prepared for chapter VI, project 1.
2. As you see the picture of Paul in II Timothy just before his death, what facts impress you most?
3. Prepare a list of standards for church leaders, based on these Pastoral Epistles and applicable for today's situations.

4. Describe the dangers facing the Church in Paul's day in present-day terminology and as though affecting your own church.

5. To develop your ability to summarize Bible truths, prepare your own outline for each of these three books.

Suggested Resources

GUTHRIE, DONALD. *The Pastoral Epistles: Tyndale New Testament Commentaries.* Grand Rapids: Eerdmans Publishing Co., 1957.

KENT, HOMER A., JR. *The Pastoral Epistles.* Winona Lake, IN: BMH Books, 1982.

CHAPTER TEN

The Church and Suffering

James, Hebrews, and I Peter

BACKGROUND There were periods during the first century when the Church, in one place or another, felt the pangs of suffering and hardship. These trials came from various sources and, to some extent, for different reasons. Nevertheless, they were equally distressing and the Christians were at times perplexed as to the purpose of all these things in their experience.

If James is rightly dated at about A.D. 45, and thus the earliest book in the New Testament, it reflects trial in the Church not long after the time of its inception (Acts 2). It describes trials from without (1:2) and within (1:13-15); recalls suffering as seen in earlier days by the prophets and Job (5:10, 11); and exhorts the suffering one to pray (5:13). The book, apparently meant for Jewish converts of the Dispersion (1:1), is really a treatise on the faith that endures in the face of all types of obstacles.

Hebrews, too, written to Jewish converts, makes references to the sufferings of believers. Written at a later date than James (probably shortly before A.D. 70), it is an exhortation to Christians to press forward, to endure, even in the face of serious pressures (cf. 12:3 ff.). Whether or not it was written in or near Rome, it reflects the serious conditions existing at that time, near the end of the reign of Nero.

First Peter, to a much greater degree than the other letters, is also concerned with this problem. The word "suffering" occurs seventeen times, being used both of the sufferings of Christ and His people. Particularly in 4:12-19, the problem is reflected. By this time (about A.D. 63-65) the pressure of Nero's persecution of the Roman Christians may have been felt in some of the provinces as well (cf. 1:1), or at least the threat was present. Thus, Peter writes to give hope by furnishing a proper perspective (cf. 1:6-9).

James

SUGGESTED READING   James

Unquestionably James is one of the most "down-to-earth" books in the New Testament. The writer is dealing with the everyday affairs, covering such matters as one's speech, business ventures, the respect of persons, disagreements between Christian brethren, relations between employers and employees, and a number of other such things. Here are problems that touch our lives continually. The teaching of James, then, is designed to show the ways in which one's faith in God is not only tested to determine its genuineness, but applied to every area of human life.

AUTHOR   The writer of the book identifies himself as "James, a servant of God and of the Lord Jesus" (1:1). As a number of men by this same name appear in the New Testament, brief consideration should be given to the problem. James, the son of Zebedee and the brother of John, was among the original disciples of the Lord Jesus. He, however, was beheaded by Herod Agrippa I (Acts 12:1, 2), before the year A.D. 44, thus would not play a part in the history of the Jerusalem church during the time under consideration. James the son of Alphaeus was also one of Jesus' disciples (Matt. 10:3), but is not otherwise referred to in the narrative. Another of our Lord's disciples, Judas (not Iscariot), had a father whose name was James (Luke 6:16). But the only prominent figure by this name who continued through this period is the man called by Paul, "James, the Lord's brother" (Gal. 1:19). He appears in the Gospels as one of the four brothers of Christ (Matt. 13:55) and, during His ministry, an unbeliever (John 7:5). He is seen, however, as a believer, in the Jerusalem prayer meeting (Acts 1:14, cf. I Cor. 15:7) and upon Peter's departure from Jerusalem, he assumes the leadership of the church there (Acts 12:17). A comparison of Galatians 2:9 with Acts 15:13-29 marks him as one of the pillars of the church. His final appearance in the New Testament is in Acts 21:18. According to tradition, he was martyred by the Jews in Jerusalem in A.D. 62.

Traditionally, this last individual of the four has been known as the writer of the epistle which bears his name. He was a very devout man, deeply concerned about the careful regulation of the life of one who professed to believe in God. Known also as a man of prayer, he urged the same exercise upon his readers (cf. 5:16-18). His outlook is much the same as that found in the teaching of our Lord. Especially notable is the close similarity between this epistle and "the Sermon on the Mount" (Matt. 5—7).

What is faith? That is the question which James attempts to answer. And it is neither an academic nor an irrelevant inquiry. It is one which pierces to the depths of one's heart and to the center of his workaday world.

OUTLINE

PURPOSE AND   Surely it is worthy of notice that in an epistle dealing
CONTENT   much with testing and suffering that the opening words
                    include "all joy" (1:2). Similar features occur in Paul's
writings, with his emphasis on "joy" and "thanksgiving" in all kinds of
circumstances (cf. also I Pet. 1:6).

The chief purpose of trial is that it might bring about endurance (the
literal meaning of "patience" in this passage) and completeness (1:3, 4).
The word "temptation" (or, "trial") here has reference to outward pressures
which bear hard upon the Christian. They are there by God's permission,
designed to test (or prove) his faith and, when overcome, hold promise of
reward (1:12). There is also the temptation that arises from within (1:13-
15), due to man's own sinful nature, but does not come from God.

True faith is productive. This is due to its vital character. That which is
alive is active. James discusses this important facet of truth under the subject
of "faith and works" (2:14-26). The key statement is that found in 2:14
"What doth it profit, my brethren, if a man say he hath faith, but have not
works? can that faith save him?" The expression "that faith" (ASV) has
reference, not to faith in general, but a particular kind of faith, namely that
which does not produce anything. If a man's life is barren of good works,
James is saying, we can only conclude that there is no genuine faith in God
present at all. From the human point of view, then, faith must be shown to
be known.

While this passage has often been set over against Paul's teaching about
faith (cf. Rom. 4), the two really complement, rather than contradict, each
other. In Romans, God knew that Abraham's faith was genuine because he
looked on his heart; in James, men only knew Abraham's faith was genuine
when they saw his good works as evidence. It seems that Paul himself puts
the two elements together when he writes of faith working through love
(Gal. 5:6).

James goes on from this point to show the relevance of all this to the life
of one who professes to have faith in Christ. His injunctions such as on the
use of the tongue (chap. 3), on business plans (chap. 4), and on prayer
(chap. 5) are of a most practical nature.

Hebrews

SUGGESTED READING   Hebrews

THEME   The central plea of this epistle is for the believer to "press on
            unto perfection" (6:1), not to digress or turn back to his former
ways. On the one hand, solemn warnings are interspersed throughout the
letter showing the danger of neglect, unbelief, immaturity, and apostasy.
One is not to turn away from the truth and the privileges of the Gospel. On
the other hand, the superiority of Christ is emphasized to a degree not found

in any other book in the New Testament. He stands above men, angels, and ceremonies—He is the final revelation of God (1:2) and the mediator of a new and better covenant (8:6).

AUTHORSHIP   One of the outstanding questions attached to Hebrews is the matter of authorship. The name of the author is absent from the letter, and all attempts to give a final answer have fallen short. Since about the fourth century the name of Paul has often been associated with it. One may point to the similarities with Paul's known epistles, such as the reference to Timothy (13:23); the request for prayer (13:18, 19; cf. Phil. 2:23, 24); the use of the phrase "the just shall live by faith" (10:38; cf. Rom. 1:17; Gal. 3:11), together with the great emphasis on the subject of faith.

Due to other features of the epistle, however, many have suggested other authors. The general style of the writing and the approach to the subject are not characteristically Pauline. The constant use of the Septuagint (the Greek version of the Old Testament) in quotations, the polished grammar, the view of the law as "a shadow" (10:1) rather than "a curse" (Gal. 3:13), look away from Pauline authorship. Thus the names of Barnabas, Luke, and Apollos have all been suggested by scholars in early or later times. Usually such discussions end with the use of the famous statement by Origen of Alexandria (3rd century): "Who it was that wrote the epistle, God alone knows certainly."

Despite the uncertainty as to the human author, the grandeur of the epistle remains unmarred. It is a matchless presentation of the glories of Christ, the Redeemer, High Priest, and Changeless One (cf. 1:3; 2:17; 4:14-16; 7:25; 10:11-13; 13:8). The superiority of Christ and of the life of faith constitute the dual theme of the book.

OUTLINE
    I. The Superiority of Christ, 1:1—10:18
       A. Above the prophets, 1:1-3
       B. Above the angels, 1:4-14; 2:5-18
           First warning: neglect, 2:1-4
       C. Above Moses, 3:1-6
           Second warning: unbelief, 3:7-19
       D. Above Joshua, 4:2-10
           Third warning: unbelief, 4:1, 11-13
       E. Above Aaron, 4:14—5:10
           Fourth warning; immaturity, 5:11—6:20
       F. Above the Levitical Priesthood, 7:1-28
       G. Above the Old Covenant, 8:1-13
       H. Above the Ordinances and Sacrifices, 9:1—10:18
   II. The Superiority of Faith, 10:19—13:21
       A. The way of access to God, 10:19-25
           Fifth warning: willful sin, 10:26-31
       B. The way of life in the world, 10:32—11:40

PURPOSE AND CONTENT   The opening statement of the epistle gathers up into one the whole of the Biblical revelation. God has spoken in the prophets—the Old Testament; He has spoken in (His) Son—the New Testament. And this latter word has reached the very height of revelation, coming in One who is described as (1) Heir, (2) Creator, (3) Deity, (4) Preserver, and (5) Redeemer (1:2, 3). Now he resides at "the right hand of the majesty on high" as our High Priest (4:14).

Thus he appears as superior to the angels, for He is their Creator (1:4—2:18), to Moses and Joshua, for He is the Master over the servant (3:1—4:13), to Aaron and his successors, for He is the Great High Priest overshadowing the lesser priests (4:14—7:28). The New Covenant, of which He is mediator, is superior to the Old (8:1-13), and His sacrifice is superior to the ceremonial offerings of bulls and goats (9:1—10:18).

The second major division (10:9—13:25) concerns faith as the superior way of life. Chapters 11 and 12 are especially outstanding here. The former shows in what ways the faith of the saints of the Old Testament was tested; the latter shows why our faith is tested. The "heroes of faith" showed what it meant to walk with God, to live and die in dependance on His promises. Christ is the greatest example of all—"the author and perfecter of . . . faith" (12:2). We are to consider Him (12:3), and learn that God, in permitting trials, in chastising us, is "rearing us as His children" to bring us to maturity and, ultimately, perfection.

Along with the two major emphases of the epistle are included the warning sections. While expositors differ as to precise interpretations, none fails to recognize the serious nature of these words. All the warnings could well be summed up in the words of 12:25, "See that ye refuse not him (God) that speaketh." [2]

Generally speaking, the warnings grow more severe and more climactic as the letter proceeds. The first warns of neglect (2:1-4); the last cautions against absolute refusal to heed what God has spoken (12:25-29). In terms of descriptive language, the two most harsh may well be those of 5:11—

---

[1] The priestly and sacrificial system of the Old Testament (especially in the books of Exod. and Lev.) forms the background for a proper understanding of Heb. This is particularly true in 4:14—10:18. Christ is presented as the High Priest who has no successor (chap. 7), the Mediator of the New Covenant which has no terminal point (chap. 8), and the spotless Sacrifice who, by His once-for-all offering, has dealt with sin completely and finally (chaps. 9 and 10).

[2] See the outline for the character of each of the seven warnings.

6:20 and 10:26-31. The one who "fell away" cannot be renewed to repentance; the one who "sins willfully" after knowing the truth is left without any sacrifice for sins.[3] The antidote to such perils is given in the exhortations of the book. There are thirteen expressions in all, urging the believer to grow in faith and to press forward instead of going backward in his spiritual experience (4:1, 11, 14, 16; 6:1; 10:22, 23, 24; 12:1 twice, 28; 13:13, 15).

I Peter

SUGGESTED READING   I Peter

BACKGROUND   Written to "the elect who are sojourners of the Dispersion" (1:1), the First Epistle of Peter gives a ray of hope in the darkness to those suffering affliction and persecution. The word "suffering" is used ten times with reference to the lot of the Christian (2:19, 20; 3:14, 17; 4:1, 13, 15, 19; 5:9, 10).[4] In addition the word "trial" (or, "temptation") occurs in two crucial passages, 1:6; 4:12. What is the Christian to do and to think in the face of such conditions? Peter's answer is given by his use of the word "hope," found in 1:3, 13, 21; 3:5, 15, and by the assurance that God has a very definite purpose in permitting these difficulties in our lives.

AUTHOR   The name Peter is one already familiar to the reader of the historical books of the New Testament. He played a major part in the earthly ministry of our Lord and was the leader of the Jerusalem Church in the first twelve chapters of Acts. A fisherman of Bethsaida, close to the Sea of Galilee in northern Palestine (John 1:44), Peter was the older brother of Andrew. He was first brought to Jesus by his brother (John 1:40-42), and it was prophesied by the Lord at that time that the old, unstable Simon would one day be the new, rock-like Peter. He was called from his fishing boat to become a fisher of men (Mark 1:16-18; Luke 5:1-11). Finally, in Mark 3:13-16, he was called and chosen as one of the Twelve to accompany the Lord and to carry on an evangelistic ministry. As one of the inner circle, together with James and John, he accompanied Christ at a number of important events during his life: the raising of Jairus' daughter (Luke 8:54); the Transfiguration scene (Luke 9:28); and on the crucifixion eve in the Garden of Gethsemane (Matt. 26:37). Being overconfident regarding his undying loyalty to his Lord, he soon denied Him (John 13:

---

[3]The interpretation of these warning sections will be affected by the view one takes of the spiritual state of the recipients of the letter. Three major views are current: (1) they were only professing Christians, but never truly regenerated. Thus they were in danger of "stopping short of salvation"; (2) they were believers, but could lose salvation by failing to maintain faith in Christ; (3) they were believers who were in danger of lapsing into a life of barrenness and uselessness, thus losing any reward.

[4]It is also used with regard to Christ in 1:11; 2:21, 23; 3:18; 4:1, 13; 5:10, a total of seven times.

36-38; 18:15-27), but was afterward graciously restored to fellowship and commissioned to follow and serve Him once again (I Cor. 15:5; John 21:15-19). As the leader of the early Church in Jerusalem, he appears as a fearless preacher, defender, and administrator. That he did learn his lesson is evident from the reading of this letter, as it abounds with references to faithfulness, the care of a shepherd for the sheep, and the responsibilities of the Christian toward his Lord and his fellow Christians. Thus, out of a full life, Peter, now an old man, writes to believers who are beset by trials and sufferings. He had found the Lord sufficient; now he exhorts these people to cast all their anxieties upon Him because He cares for them (cf. 5:7).

OUTLINE

    I. Salutation, 1:1, 2
    II. Perspective and Suffering, 1:3—2:10
    III. Pressure and Suffering, 2:11—4:6
    IV. Service and Suffering, 4:7-11
    V. Witness and Suffering, 4:12-19
    VI. Personal Attitudes and Suffering, 5:1-11
    VII. Conclusion, 5:12-14

PURPOSE AND CONTENT   The Christian life is never described as a bed of roses. In fact, Peter states, amid the sufferings that were then present, "For hereunto were ye called: because Christ also suffered for you, leaving you an example, that ye should follow his steps" (2:21). For what reasons are such things permitted by the Lord? They are meant to prove our faith that we may "be found unto praise and glory and honor at the revelation of Jesus Christ" (1:7). It is actually a privilege to "suffer for righteousness' sake" (3:14); our Lord has suffered on this account (2:21; 4:1). Partaking of Christ's sufferings will result in rejoicing at His coming (4:13). There is suffering which is "according to the will of God" which is meant to bring a committal of our souls "in well-doing unto a faithful Creator" (4:19). That is to say, God knows what He is doing. We are to continue to do well despite the circumstances. We have been called as God's children to share His glory. He Himself shall "perfect, establish, strengthen you" (5:10).

Countering this emphasis is the note of hope.[5] What comfort this affords to the Christian. God has begotten us "unto a living hope" (1:3), and has reserved an inheritance for us in heaven (1:4), and is guarding us in view of that day (1:5). Our hope is on the grace of God, and on God Himself (1:13, 21; 3:5). Even as He raised Christ from the dead, so we also shall be caught up to glory. The hope within us, being laid hold of by faith, becomes so real that people around us inquire concerning it (3:15). Thus

---

[5]Notice also the occurrences of the word "grace" in the epistle: 1:2, 10, 13; 2:19, 20 "acceptable"; 3:7; 4:10 "gift"; 5:5, 10, 12.

the very hardships we face become opportunities for witnessing for Christ.

Peter's use of the imperative mood of the verb in his epistle is noteworthy, together with participles used in the sense of commands. By such devices he has attempted to impress upon his readers that living for God makes real demands upon us. This positive injunction is to guide us and form us unto the day of His appearing.[6] It is an application of Christ's word in the second Gospel, "Thou shalt love the Lord thy God with all thy heart, and with all thy soul, and with all thy mind, and with all thy strength . . . (and) thou shalt love thy neighbor as thyself" (Mark 12:30, 31). We show our love by obeying His commands (cf. I Pet. 1:22).

Suggested Questions and Discussions

1. On what important subject is James a treatise?
2. According to James, what are some of the aspects of daily living which should be affected by our faith?
3. Give a brief background of the probable writer of the book of James.
4. Compare and show the relationship of James' teaching on faith with Paul's teaching on the subject in Romans 4.
5. In what ways is the book of Hebrews similar to Paul's known epistles?
6. What is the dual theme of the book of Hebrews?
7. To whom is Christ considered superior in the book of Hebrews?
8. Briefly summarize the ministry of Peter prior to Christ's death.
9. Summarize Peter's teaching concerning suffering as found in I Peter.

Additional Exploration

1. Compare and contrast the lives of Peter and James.
2. What important lessons should be learned from the warnings of Hebrews?
3. List a number of practical problems found in most Christians' lives which are answered in these epistles. Indicate where each answer is found.
4. To understand more fully the differences between law and grace or faith and works, expand project 2 of chapter VII by indicating specific contrasts between them in the book of Hebrews.
5. Prepare a summary of the character and ministry of Christ as presented in the book of Hebrews. *OR* Expand your chart prepared for chapter I, project 1.
6. List the characteristics of today's true Christian as portrayed in these epistles.

Suggested Resources

KENT, HOMER A., JR. *The Epistle to the Hebrews.* Grand Rapids: Baker Book House, 1972.
STIBBS, A. M. *The First Epistle of Peter: Tyndale New Testament Commentaries.* Grand Rapids: Eerdmans Publishing Co., 1959.
TASKER, R. V. G. *The General Epistle of James: Tyndale New Testament Commentaries.* Grand Rapids: Eerdmans Publishing Company, 1957.

---

[6]There are over thirty such statements in this short epistle. *See* M. C. Tenney, *New Testament Survey,* rev. ed., pp. 351, 352.

CHAPTER ELEVEN

The Church and
False Teaching
II Peter, Jude,
I, II, and III John

BACKGROUND The last five New Testament Epistles, three of them containing only one brief chapter each, are linked together by their common concern with false teaching in the realm of Christian doctrine and ethics. Second Peter and Jude warn of those who scorn the authority of the Lord and His Word. Like false teachers in the Old Testament, they will taste the judgment of God coming upon them. The three letters ascribed to John, though they, like Hebrews, are anonymous, are written against the malignant influence of Gnosticism, which at this date (late first century) was beginning to show itself as a system of teaching. Professing to possess superior, mystic knowledge leading to salvation, their teaching set forth strange views of Christ and the nature of creation. John calls it "the spirit of antichrist" (I John 4:1-3).

II Peter

SUGGESTED READING   II Peter

AUTHORSHIP The early Church was slow in acknowledging II Peter to be on the same level with the other books which came to compose the New Testament canon. A number of contrasts with I Peter are readily noticed, such as the lack of specific address (as in I Pet. 1:1), the rough grammatical character and style of writing, and in addition, the striking similarities of language between chapter 2 and the Epistle of Jude. Yet it should be remembered that the book was recognized as canonical by the Council of Laodicea in A.D. 363 and the Council of Carthage in A.D. 397.

Much more definite is the internal evidence for Petrine authorship. The writer calls himself "Simon Peter, a servant and apostle of Jesus Christ" (1:1). The name Simon (or, Simeon) is reminiscent of his original name (cf. John 1:42; Acts 15:14). There are many autobiographical references in the letter. He recalls the Transfiguration experience (1:16-18; cf. Mark 9:2-8). He uses a fisherman's word in 2:14, 18, "enticing." In 3:1, he makes reference to this letter as "the second epistle" he had written to these readers. Further, he is one with his readers in having obtained like precious faith.

THEME   The key word of the epistle is "knowledge," which in its various forms occurs twelve times (1:2, 3, 5, 6, 8, 16, 20; 2:20, 21; 3:3, 17, 18). In a letter which aims to combat false teaching, the knowledge of the truth is the key idea. Together with this, Peter stresses the importance of remembering certain things (1:12, 13; 3:1) and shows the danger of forgetting important truths (1:9; 3:8). Thus, throughout the letter, the teachings of the Word of God are represented as true and normative for the Christian life.

OUTLINE

      I. Introduction, 1:1, 2
     II. Knowledge and the Christian Life, 1:3-11
    III. Knowledge and the Word of God, 1:12-21
    IV. Knowledge and the False Teaching, 2:1-22
     V. Knowledge and the Second Coming, 3:1-13
   VI. Conclusion: Steadfastness and Growth, 3:14-18

PURPOSE AND   God has made full provision for the spiritual life of the
CONTENT   believer (1:3). Thus, the believer's responsibility is to avail himself of the divine resources so that he will be neither "idle nor unfruitful unto the knowledge of our Lord Jesus Christ" (1:8). This is Peter's opening thought in the epistle and by means of these statements he has prepared the way for his main arguments.

First, the Word of God given by the Holy Spirit (1:20, 21) is that to which we should give heed (1:19). Because its source is divine, its message is authoritative. It should be stressed that the chief thrust of the statement in 1:20, 21, is regarding the *origin,* not the meaning, of Scripture. It came not "by the will of man" but "by the Holy Spirit."

Second, the path taken by the false teachers, who deny "even the Master that bought them," leads toward certain judgment (2:1) and "the last state is become worse with them than the first" (2:20). Those who follow them can expect nothing better. The sure judgment of God upon the sinners of the Old Testament (2:4, 5, 6, 15) is a solemn warning to all.

Third, the Second Coming of Christ will be God's vindication of His Name and purpose, and "the day of the Lord" will be the day of judgment for the scoffers of the world (chap. 3). Those who deny the reality of this event forget "this one thing," says Peter, "that one day is with the Lord as a thousand years, and a thousand years as one day" (3:8). Only because He is longsuffering, "not wishing that any should perish," do the scoffers even remain to carry on their false ways (3:9).

This final message leaves a challenge with the readers of the letter. "Wherefore, beloved, seeing that ye look for these things, give diligence that ye may be found in peace, without spot and blameless in his sight . . . But grow in the grace and knowledge of our Lord and Saviour Jesus Christ. To him be the glory both now and for ever" (3:14, 18).

Jude

SUGGESTED READING   Jude

The letter that was to have been written concerning "our common faith" turned out, by constraint upon the writer, to be an exhortation "to contend earnestly for the faith" (v. 3). One of the chief differences between Jude and II Peter seems to be that while Peter warned that "there shall be false teachers" (2:1), Jude states that "there are certain men crept in privily" (v. 4). One anticipates the problem, while the other realizes it as present. Apparently, then, this epistle is somewhat later than II Peter. If Peter is dated about A.D. 65-67, Jude might be placed at A.D. 75-85.

AUTHOR   Jude was a "brother of James," and seems to fit into the pattern sketched earlier (cf. chap. X on James). One of the brothers of Christ and of James was named Jude (Matt. 13:55). They appear as believers in Acts 1:14, and he writes now as "a servant of Jesus Christ" (1:1).

THEME   As he begins to write, he uses the interesting expression, "the faith which was once for all delivered unto the saints" (v. 3).[1] Here "the faith" has reference to "the body of doctrine," held in common by the church at that time. There is a note of finality about it—"which was once for all delivered." God has committed the Gospel to the Church to be kept inviolate, as a trust (cf. Gal. 1:6-9; I Tim. 1:19; 6:3, 20, 21, II Tim. 1:13, 14). Doctrine, however, is not to be held in detachment from life. Correctness of teaching must result in holiness of living, else the practical purpose is lost. This is the error which Jude combats a kind of antinomianism, or "lawless libertinism" (v. 4), which results in a denial of the rightful place of Christ in the life of the individual.

OUTLINE
    I. Salutation, 1, 2
    II. Exhortation: Defense of the Faith, 3, 4
    III. Illustration: Departures from the Faith, 5-16
    IV. Admonition: Progress in the Faith, 17-23
    V. Conclusion: A Doxology, 24, 25

PURPOSE AND CONTENT   Jude, along with II Peter 2, turns to the Old Testament for illustrations of godlessness and makes clear God's judgment upon all such persons. A comparison of the two is as follows.

---

[1]The same word is used to characterize the redemptive work of Christ in Heb. 9:12; 10:10.

Jude		II Peter 2	
Israel in the wilderness	(v. 5)	———	
The angels who fell	(v. 6)	The angels who fell	(v. 4)
———		The Antediluvians	(v. 5)
Sodom and Gomorrah	(v. 7)	Sodom and Gomorrah	(v. 6)
The way of Cain	(v. 11)	———	
The error of Balaam	(v. 11)	The way of Balaam	(v. 15)
The disputing of Korah	(v. 11)	———	

Jude employed these illustrations for a number of specific reasons.

First, he used them as a means of informing his readers of the serious consequences of unbelief. Israel illustrates *unbelief* (v. 5); the fallen angels illustrate *disobedience* (v. 6); Sodom and Gomorrah illustrate *moral defilement* (v. 7).

Second, he thus depicted the character of the false teachers of whom he warns his readers. Cain is a picture of *willfulness,* Balaam of *greed,* and Korah of *presumption* (v. 11).[2]

Third, by way of anticipation, Jude tells what will be the end of the false teachers. Using a quotation from the Jewish work, *The Book of Enoch,* he illustrates what God will do to these "ungodly sinners" (vv. 14, 15).

In the face of all such dangers, the personal responsibility of the believers is to (1) remember the apostles' teaching (v. 17) and (2) keep yourselves in the love of God (v. 21). This latter injunction is linked with a number of participial clauses: (a) building yourselves up on your most holy faith (v. 20), (b) praying in the Holy Spirit (v. 20), (c) looking for mercy of our Lord Jesus Christ unto eternal life (v. 21). Along with these, his responsibility to others is (1) to have mercy on some (v. 22, 23) and (2) to save some out of the fire (v. 23).

I John

SUGGESTED READING   I John

BACKGROUND   John writes against the Gnostics who denied the reality of our Lord's humanity as well as His deity. His epistles, especially the first, are powerful weapons against such heresies, whether in old or modern dress.

This letter is closely related to his Gospel (see chap. IV). Both concern the Lord Jesus and the eternal life which comes to those who trust in Him (John 20:30, 31; I John 5:13). The former gives the declaration of salvation; the latter the assurance of it. Both speak of "the Word," the term used for Christ as the revealer of God.[3] The vocabulary of the books is similar,

---

[2] Jude also includes the devil as an example of *blasphemy* (vv. 9, 10), although the incident is not included in any O. T. book. It is taken from a Jewish inter-testamental work, and is used here as a graphic illustration of his characterization of the false teachers.

[3] Even as the spoken word reveals the thought of the person, so the Lord Jesus revealed the Father (cf. John 1:18; I John 1:1, 2).

both employing such important words as "beginning" cf. 1:1 in each); "witness" (33 times in John, 6 times in I John); "believe" (98 times and 9 times); "eternal life" (John 3:15; I John 1:2); "love" (John 3:16; I John 4:9); "abide" (John 15:4; I John 2:28); and many others.

All of John's writings are usually dated near the end of the first century, somewhere between A.D. 85-95. Thus, as an old man, he looks back to his experiences with his Lord, upon which he had long meditated, and also at the current problems of the Church.

PURPOSE AND CONTENT John writes to define the nature of the person of Christ in the face of heretical teachings which were afflicting the Church near the end of the first century. The general name given to this teaching was Gnosticism, a religio-philosophic school which was basically characterized by the idea that only spirit was good and matter was evil. As in other Greek and Oriental religious systems, the Gnostics believed that one must free himself from the material world and be occupied alone with spirit. The way of escape, for the Gnostics, was the way of superior knowledge. By learning the mysterious secrets of the universe, the initiate of the cult could supposedly attain freedom.

With regard to the teachings of Christianity, the opposition of this heresy centered in the person of Christ. Obviously, if matter (which involved the human body) was evil, God could not be "manifest in the flesh," else He would be defiled. Therefore, Christ's humanity was not real; the disciples only saw a phantom; He only seemed to be real. If, as others taught, Jesus was truly man, the "Christ-spirit" did not actually unite with Him, except for the brief time between the baptism and the crucifixion.[4] This was, therefore, a denial of His deity.

When one becomes aware of these prevalent false claims, many of John's statements in the First Epistle take on new meaning. John combats Docetism by his insistence on the reality of the humanity of Christ (1:1-3; 4:1-3). He utters severe words against Cerinthianism by emphasizing the fact that Jesus is the Christ, the Son of God (1:3, 7; 2:22, 23; 3:23; 4:15; 5:1, 20). This epistle should serve as a final answer to a heresy which persists until the present day.

The primary purpose of the epistle, as stated by John himself, is given in 5:13: "These things have I written unto you, that ye may know that ye have eternal life, *even* unto you that believe on the name of the Son of God." His remarks are addressed to "the children of God," those who have been "begotten of God." Thus it is a family letter and the word *fellowship* is used

---

[4]The former of these beliefs was called Docetism from the Greek word *dokeo*, "to seem (to be);" the latter Cerinthianism, after the name of its champion, Cerinthus. Tradition informs us that John knew Cerinthus and regarded him as an enemy of the Gospel.

by John to describe the ideal relationship between God and His children (cf. 1:3, 6, 7).

OUTLINE

CHARACTERISTIC FEATURES In this letter, John describes God as "light" (1:5) and "love" (4:8). The one has reference to his holiness (cf. James 1:17) and is meant to stress to the believer the need for properly dealing with any sin in his life, that is, anything that would prevent fellowship with his Father. In 1:5—2:2 the remedy is given. The blood of Christ is the *basis* for cleansing (1:7); confession on the part of the believer is the *condition* for cleansing (1:9); forgiveness by God is the *accompaniment* of cleansing (1:9). Those who deny the presence of a sin nature (1:8) only deceive themselves; those who deny they have committed acts of sin (1:10) make God a liar.

The other descriptive word, "love," has reference to God's attitude toward us, as well as being descriptive of His nature. (cf. 4:9). We learn the meaning of love by seeing what God has done for us (4:10). Thus, we are not only to love Him, but one another also (4:11).

Notice that John, as he writes, makes use of many contrasting terms and ideas. Things are "either black or white." He speaks in terms of "one or the other." Such passages as 1:6, 7; 2:4, 5; 2:9, 10; 2:17; 2:22, 23; 3:10; 3:18; 4:2, 3; 4:20; and 5:12 are outstanding examples of his technique. His epistle is written to enable us to put our profession to the test.

Only in John among the New Testament writers does the now familiar expression "antichrist" occur. It is introduced in I John 2:18, then appears in 2:22; 4:3; and II John 7. The meaning of anti is "one who takes the place of," or "one who stands against (or, opposes)." The essence of the nature of the antichrist is the denial of the rightful place of the Father and the Son; he himself would be supreme in the world. Furthermore, the spirit of antichrist is a denial of the reality of Christ's incarnation, thus attempting to do away with his redemptive work, by which also He laid "the sentence of death" upon Satan himself (cf. Heb. 2:14). "And we know that the Son of God is come, and hath given us an understanding, that we may know him that is true, and we are in him that is true, even in his Son" (I John 5:20).

II John

SUGGESTED READING   II John

PURPOSE AND   This, together with III John, seems to be a sampling of
CONTENT   John's personal correspondence. Both letters are addressed to individuals and have to do with a number of personal matters.

The key word of the letter is "truth." John stresses the need for "walking
in the truth" because "many deceivers are gone forth into the world." He
who denies the doctrine of Christ is not to be given Christian greetings (vv.
10, 11), lest we find ourselves "partaking in his evil works."

OUTLINE

I. Salutation, 1-3
II. Walking in the Truth, 4-11
   A. The commandment of the Father, 4-6
   B. The message of the deceivers, 7-11
III. Conclusion, 12, 13

III John

SUGGESTED READING   III John

PURPOSE AND   The recipient of this final epistle of John is called only
CONTENT   "Gaius the beloved" (v. 1). He is identified no further,
                   so must have been well-known to the members of the
Asian churches where John served during the last years of his life. The
name itself was a familiar one, often appearing in the writings of Paul,
where we see Gaius (of Corinth) in Romans 16:23, Paul's host in that city;
Gaius of Macedonia in Acts 19:29; and Gaius of Derbe in Acts 20:4.

Its key word is "hospitality." The letter recognizes the kindnesses of
Gaius in showing "an open door" to Christian workers and strangers alike
(v. 5) and encourages him to continue this ministry (v. 6).

The troublesome Diotrephes, who brazenly excommunicated those in the
church who did not recognize his "preeminence," John promises to discipline when he comes (vv. 9, 10). By way of contrast, the man Demetrius is
commended by all in the church (v. 12). His commendation, "good report
of all men, and of the truth itself," challenges the Christian to walk in truth.

OUTLINE

I. Salutation, 1
II. Prayer for Gaius' Health, 2-4
III. Praise for Gaius' Hospitality, 5-8
IV. Condemnation of Diotrephes' Policy, 9-11
V. Commendation of Demetrius' Character, 12
VI. Conclusion, 13

Suggested Questions and Discussions

1. What emphasis is common among the last five New Testament Epistles?
2. How is the theme of II Peter emphasized by the writer?
3. What is the teaching of II Peter concerning the Scriptures?
4. Compare II Peter and Jude in reference to their statements concerning false teachers.
5. What illustrations of Old Testament godlessness are used by both Peter and Jude?
6. Compare the similarities of emphases by John in I John and his Gospel.
7. Justify calling I John a family letter.
8. What attitudes and teachings characterize the spirit of antichrist?
9. What was John's purpose in writing II and III John?

Additional Exploration

1. Show from I John the tests by which a person today can know whether or not he is truly a Christian.
2. Compare present-day error with Gnosticism and indicate how I John provides answers for those denying Christ's deity or bodily existence.
3. From II Peter and I John, expand your findings on the true Christian in chapter X, project 6.
4. Without the use of aids, prepare an outline for one of the epistles studied in this chapter.

Suggested Resources

GREEN, M. *Second Epistle General of Peter and the General Epistle of Jude: Tyndale New Testament Commentaries.* Grand Rapids: Eerdmans Publishing Co., 1968.

MARSHALL, I. H. *The Epistles of John: New International Commentary on the New Testament.* Grand Rapids: Eerdmans Publishing Co., 1978.

STOTT, JOHN R. *The Epistles of John: Tyndale New Testament Commentaries.* Grand Rapids: Eerdmans Publishing Co., 1964.

CHAPTER TWELVE

Book of the Revelation

SUGGESTED READING   Revelation

The book of the Revelation, like the book of Daniel in the Old Testament, is apocalyptic. The term means "to unveil" or "to uncover;" thus, "to reveal" something which has been beforehand veiled, covered, or hidden.

CHARACTERISTICS OF   Several characteristics of apocalyptic writ-
APOCALYPTIC WRITINGS   ings are worthy of mention:

Usually written in times of trouble and distress

This is seen in both Daniel and Revelation. In one, the days of the Babylonian captivity are vividly portrayed; in the other, the beginnings of the conflict between the Roman Empire and the Church.

Convey their message by means of signs, symbols, dreams, and visions

John writes in Revelation 1:1 that his message was "sent and signified" (i.e., portrayed by the use of "signs," or, physical figures having spiritual meanings attached to them). Within the framework of four great visions, John presents the main outlines of his message.

Give promise of the eventual triumph of good over evil

By the appearance of the kingdom of God, together with the heavenly Lord (cf. "King of Kings and Lord of Lords," Rev. 19:16) as the Sovereign Ruler of the creation, all things shall be subjected to His will (cf. Dan. 2:44; Rev. 11:15).

Despite the fact that the Revelation seems to many strange and foreboding, and thus is often neglected, the Revelation is the only book in the New Testament containing the promise of blessing to the one "that readeth, and they that hear the words of the prophecy, and keep the things that are written therein" (1:3; cf. Josh. 1:7, 8). In addition, the book closes with a serious warning to any who would add to or take away from the contents of the prophecy (22:18, 19). Above all, it must be emphasized that this book is, according to its own statement, "the Revelation of Jesus Christ, which God gave him to show unto his servants" (1:1). With such character attached to it by so plain a statement, the contents are worthy of the diligent study of every believer.

BACKGROUND   By a reading of the book itself, one sees readily that persecution and trouble were already threatening the Church. Both from without and within serious problems were in evidence. The church of Ephesus was commended for her endurance and discernment of evil men (2:2); the church of Smyrna would have tribulation ten days (2:10); in Pergamum, Antipas was martyred (2:13); "great tribulation" hung over Thyatira (2:22); the church in Philadelphia was promised the Lord's protection amid the hour of trial (3:10).

The date of the writing of Revelation was about A.D. 90-95. During the first century, the Roman emperors held sway over the world, from Augustus to Domitian. All the Roman persecutions before the days of the Emperor Decius (A.D. 250) were local in nature. The Christians in certain places began to feel the sting of official opposition in A.D. 64, then again, it seems, during Domitian's time. The exile of John to Patmos was just one example of the present and impending tribulations spoken of within the Revelation (1:9).

Would this be the lot of the Church forever? Was it possible that Satan and his evil agents would win the victory? The book gives a decisive answer. The dragon would be cast down from heaven (12:9); the saints would overcome him (12:11). Eventually, he and his kind would be cast into "the lake of fire" (19:20; 20:10). Thus, God would be supreme and the Church established forever, as "a bride adorned for her husband" (21:2). Even as the Lord Jesus had said, so it would be: "the gates of Hades shall not prevail against it" (Matt. 16:18).

METHODS OF   Before attempting to investigate the details of the
INTERPRETATION   book, it is necessary to establish some method or
                                  methods of approaching it. Bible scholars recognize
four basic methods.

The Preterist Method

Having reference to past time, this approach asserts that the events in the Revelation belong to the first century, and have, therefore, long ago been fulfilled. There is no prophetic or future aspect to the book. The setting for the visions was the existing conflict between the Church and Rome in the age of the apostles (i.e., up to A.D. 100), according to the preterist method of interpretation.

This view emphasizes the relevance of the book to the churches to which it was written (1:11), but it hardly seems in keeping with the professed forward look of John's message which specifically presents predictions of things to come. (cf. 1:3, 19; 22:18, 19).

The Historicist Method

Giving full recognition to the relation of the drama of the book to earthly events, this approach sees the Revelation as "a picture book" of the conflict between the Church and the world (energized by Satan) from the time of the apostles until the end of the age. The crises which have arisen in world history, the aspiring world-conquerors of past and present are portrayed herein—and all are doomed to failure.

The major weakness of this method is the difficulty in equating events of the book with events in history. Serious, and apparently irreconcilable, disagreements of a major sort between those who hold the view cast doubt upon the validity of the approach as a single solution to the book. Yet it does stress the tangency of the message to the realm of human history.

The Futurist Method

With the exception of chapters 1—3, the Revelation is viewed as wholly future, depicting the drama which awaits the end of the age, the day of God's wrath and the appearance of Christ from heaven. The opening section of the book, the letters to the seven Churches (chaps. 1—3), is either regarded as limited to the first century, or as a kind of sevenfold, symbolic sketch of the spiritual history of the Church from the Apostolic Age to the Second Advent.

In view of the prophetic language of the book (4:1) and the magnitude of the events predicted in chapters 4—22, this method seems to do greater justice to the interpretation than the previous methods. Yet the possible danger is that the book is thus rendered irrelevant to the first-century recipients of its message and, in a sense, to anyone prior to the end of the age itself. If this tendency is guarded against, the futurist method is of great value.

The Idealist Method

This method should be distinguished from the three that have been discussed in that it is not tied to history, that is, the occurrence of literal events. It deals with spiritual, rather than historical, realities. Emphasizing the conflict between God and Satan, good and evil, righteousness and sin, it assures the reader, apart from concern with specific historical situations, that the victory will be won by the forces of right.

Certainly the spirit of the book has been caught by the idealist approach, but the virtual elimination of the historical setting is hardly in keeping with the Biblical teaching of God's activity within the realm of human history. The symbolic element should not be the single emphasis; the predictive aspect must be maintained.

None of these approaches to the interpretation of this prophecy is singularly satisfactory. An attempt has been made to state concisely the strengths and weaknesses of all the methods, thus enabling the student to cull from each the useful features and use them wisely in his own study. In this task, as in all Bible study, the guidance of the Holy Spirit is essential (I Cor. 2:6-16; cf. James 1:5).

STRUCTURE OF THE BOOK   In analyzing the Revelation with regard to its structure, notice that John uses a key phrase four times, thus dividing the book into major divisions based upon four visions which he saw. The phrase is "in the Spirit," and occurs in 1:10; 4:2; 17:3; and 21:10. It is used in the Old Testament of the prophets as they experienced the revelatory ministry of the Holy Spirit, conveying to them the Word of God (cf. Ezek. 3:12; 37:1). The chart which follows will aid in identifying the visions as they appear throughout the book.

The Visions of John

Reference	Location	Vision	Content
1:9— 3:22	Patmos	One like unto a Son of man	Christ as Lord amidst His Churches
4:1—16:21	Heaven	The Throne and the Lamb	Christ as the Lamb; Wrath of God
17:1—21:8	Wilderness	Woman and the Beast	Christ as King of Kings and Victor over His enemies
21:9—22:6	Mountain	The New Jerusalem	Christ as Bridegroom with His Bride in Glory

OUTLINE   The outline for the book is built around the four visions, together with the introduction (1:1-8) and the conclusion (22:6-21). It emphasizes the centrality of Christ throughout the entire portrayal.

    I. Introduction, 1:1-8
   II. The First Vision: Christ and the Seven Churches, 1:9—3:22
  III. The Second Vision: Christ and the Earth-Judgments, 4:1—16:21
      A. The throne in Heaven and the Lamb, 4:1—5:14
      B. The seven seals opened, 6:1—8:5
      C. The seven trumpets sounded, 8:6—11:19
      D. The beasts and their warfare, 12:1—14:20
      E. The seven bowls poured out, 15:1—16:21
  IV. The Third Vision: Christ and His Victories, 17:1—21:8
      A. The fall of Babylon the Great, 17:1—18:24
      B. The joy in Heaven, 19:1-10
      C. The appearance of Christ, 19:11-16
      D. The defeat of the Beast, 19:17-21
      E. The binding of Satan, 20:1-3
      F. The Millennium, 20:4-6
      G. The final rebellion and judgment, 20:7-15
      H. The new Heaven and the new earth, 21:1-8
   V. The Fourth Vision: Christ and His Bride, 21:9—22:5
  VI. Conclusion: Final Exhortations and Benediction, 22:6-21

An Analysis of the Letters to the Seven Churches of Asia
REVELATION 2—3

Church	Ephesus 2:1-7	Smyrna 2:8-11	Pergamum 2:12-17	Thyatira 2:18-29	Sardis 3:1-6	Philadelphia 3:7-13	Laodicea 3:14-22
Character of Christ	Sovereign Lord 2:1	Risen Lord 2:8	Warring Lord 2:12, 16	Judging Lord 2:18	Omniscient Lord 3:1	Authoritative Lord 3:7	Divine Lord 3:14
Commendation	Orthodoxy 2:2	Endurance 2:9	Faithfulness 2:13	Industry 2:19	(none)	Endurance 3:10	(none)
Condemnation	Coldness 2:4	(none)	False Teaching 2:14, 15	Unfaithfulness 2:20	Unreality 3:1	(none)	Lukewarmness 3:15, 16
Counsel	Remember, repent, repeat first works 2:5	Be watchful unto death 2:10	Repent 2:16	Repent; hold fast 2:22, 25	Be watchful; remember, repent 3:2, 3	Hold fast 3:11	Buy gold, garments, eyesalve 3:18, 19
Caution	Removal 2:5	(none)	War 2:16	Death 2:23	Invasion 3:3	(none)	Separation 3:16
Covenant with overcomer	Eat of the tree of life 2:7	Not hurt by the second death 2:11	Hidden manna, White stone, new name 2:17	Rulership; morning star 2:26-28	White garments; name kept and confessed 3:5	New position; new name 3:12	Share Christ's throne 3:21

The Three Series of Judgments

	Seal Judgments	Trumpet Judgments	Vial Judgments
1	6:1, 2 Rider on a white horse Carried a bow Wore a crown Object: To conquer	8:7 Hail, fire and blood on the earth Result: ⅓ part earth, ⅓ part trees, all green grass burned up	16:2 Poured into earth Result: Noisome and grievous sore upon worshipers of the beast
2	6:3, 4 Rider on a red horse Carried a great sword Object: To take peace from the earth	8:8, 9 Fiery mountain cast into the sea Result: ⅓ of sea blood, ⅓ of sea creatures die, ⅓ of ships destroyed	16:3 Poured into the sea Result: All sea-life died
3	6:5, 6 Rider on a black horse Carried a balance Object: Produce famine conditions	8:10, 11 Burning star falls upon earth—named Wormwood Result: ⅓ of waters made bitter; many men die	16:4-7 Poured in rivers and sources of waters Result: Water became blood; Revenge on murderers
4	6:7, 8 Rider on a pale horse Death followed by Hades Object: To kill by sword, famine, death and wild beasts	8:12 Celestial disturbances Result: ⅓ of heavenly bodies darkened; day and night affected	16:8, 9 Poured upon the sun Result: Men scorched with fire; blasphemed God
5	6:9-11 Souls of martyrs under the altar Object: To cry for revenge against their murderers	9:1-11 Star (ruler) falls to earth; opens the pit; locusts emerge led by Apollyon Result: Men tormented 5 months; unable to die	16:10, 11 Poured upon the throne of the beast Result: Kingdom darkened; men in pain; did not repent
6	6:12-17 Seismic and celestial disturbances Object: Day of God's wrath upon the earth	9:13-22 Four angels at Euphrates released; armies of horsemen proceed Result: ⅓ of men killed by horses which breathe fire, smoke and brimstone	16:12-16 Poured upon Euphrates River Result: River dried up. Eastern kings advance to Har-Mageddon (Armageddon)
7	8:1, 2 Silence in heaven for a half-hour Object: Preparation for sounding of seven trumpets	11:15-19 Great voices in Heaven, and 24 elders sing praise to God Result: God's kingdom supreme over the earth	16:17-21 Poured upon the air Result: Voice announces "It is done"; disturbances and plague of hail; men blaspheme God

The first vision, in one sense, is easier to understand than those which follow. As the Lord speaks to John (1:9-20) and then to the Seven Churches (chaps. 2, 3), we find language which, within the context of first-century conditions, is relatively clear. That which is emphasized here is the sovereignty of the Head as He walks among the lampstands (the Churches) and holds the seven stars (the messengers, or leaders, of the Churches) within His right hand, the place of authority and honor.

The seven churches of Asia, selected from a greater number then existing, are each analyzed by the Lord, and their spiritual condition is laid bare.[1] A general pattern is followed by Christ in speaking to each. Two exceptions are notable, however. Each church (as a whole) is commended except two, Sardis and Laodicea. Each church (as a whole) is condemned except two, Smyrna and Philadelphia.[2] The careful study of each letter, giving attention to the background and location of each church, the kinds of things said to each, and the spiritual counsel for the present day, will prove most rewarding.

The framework for the second vision (4:1—16:21) is the description of the three series of judgments upon the earth, each consisting of seven parts.[3] The magnitude of these events is breathtaking, and, whether interpreted literally or symbolically, they impress the reader with the fury of divine vengeance against unrepentant sinners (cf. Rom. 12:19; Heb. 10:30, 31).

In considering the three series, attention should be called to the problem of the relation of the judgments. Briefly, it is this, do they follow one another (consecutive)? Do they occur within the same period of time and end together (concurrent)? Or, do they all happen at the same time (simultaneous)? Each of the three positions has been adopted by equally sound commentators; no final solution has yet appeared.

Within this general framework occur a number of so-called "parenthetical events." They are found in 7:1-8; 7:9-17; 10:1-11; 11:1-13; 12:1-17; 13:1-18; 14:1-5; 14:6-12; 14:13; 14:14-20. These events, for the most part, appear to occur within the same time sequence as the judgments, but concentrate mainly upon persons, both human and angelic, showing their relation to the day of God's wrath.

The third vision (17:1—21:8) gives special attention to the victory of

---

[1]The accompanying chart, "An Analysis of the letters to the Seven Churches of Asia," will serve to present the characteristic words spoken by the Lord and the spiritual condition of each Church.

[2]Only these two among the seven cities are thriving communities today (although, of course, the names have been changed), and have maintained a Christian witness (Eastern Orthodox) in their locations. The Lord promised to each of them His protection and blessing because of their faithfulness. Cf. John 17:15.

[3]The chart, "The Three Series of Judgments," gives a concise, consecutive analysis of the contents of each judgment. Reading it vertically will reveal the total impact of each series; reading it horizontally will show the contrasts and comparisons between each. This latter approach is especially important in relation to the trumpet and vial series.

Christ over His enemies. In order of occurrence they are the harlot and the Beast of Babylon; the Beast and the False prophets with their followers; Satan and the rebels of earth; and unregenerate mankind. Thus the way is prepared for "the new heavens and the new earth." A crucial passage within this vision is 20:4-6, picturing the millennial reign of Christ, when He shall be vindicated upon the earth, the place of His rejection (cf. I Cor. 15:25-27). The saints shall reign with Him (cf. I Cor. 6:2), and shall exercise their function as "priests of God and of Christ."

Finally, in the fourth vision (21:9—22:5) dawns "the new heavens and the new earth." The spotless Bride of Christ stands in vivid contrast to the scarlet woman, the harlot of Babylon (chapter 17). The perfections of the New Jerusalem are portrayed by John, centered in the unbroken fellowship between God and His people. With the banishment of death and the appearance of the tree of life, the pristine beauty of Eden reappears (cf. Gen. 2). That which sin has defiled is here restored and purified. Thus God shall be "all in all." The story of redemption is completed.

Suggested Questions and Discussions

1. List and illustrate from the Revelation three outstanding characteristics of apocalyptic writings.
2. Why is this book worthy of the diligent study of every believer?
3. Within what framework does John present the main outlines of his message?
4. Give a brief background for John's writing the book of Revelation.
5. Define and comment briefly on four methods of interpreting the Revelation.
6. What three possible views concerning the judgments divide Bible scholars?
7. What enemies of Christ are defeated in Revelation 17—20 in order to prepare the way for the new heavens and the new earth?
8. Briefly summarize the blessings of Revelation 21 and 22.

Additional Exploration

1. Compare the presentation of the character of Christ in the letters to the seven churches with the depiction of Him in the Epistles.
2. Justify dividing the book into four sections on the basis of the phrase, "in the Spirit." Compare our use of the term today.
3. From your Scripture reading give a brief account of the final events and doom of the devil and his followers.
4. Write a paper of several paragraphs summarizing the message of the New Testament as it applies to your own life.

Suggested Resources

LADD, G. E. *Commentary on the Book of Revelation of John.* Grand Rapids: Eerdmans Publishing Co., 1971.

MOUNCE, R. *What Are We Waiting For?* Elgin, IL: David C. Cook Publishing Co., 1979.

RYRIE, C. C. *Revelation.* Chicago: Moody Press, 1968.

TENNEY, MERRILL C. *Interpreting Revelation.* Grand Rapids: Eerdmans Publishing Co., 1957.

WALVOORD, JOHN. *The Revelation of Jesus Christ.* Chicago: Moody Press, 1966.